AFFILIATE MANAGEMENT for Self-managed Programs

Steven Lownds

Print ISBN: 978-1-7391341-5-0
E-book ISBN: 978-1-7391341-0-5

First digital edition: October 2022
First paperback edition: October 2022

Editing by David Paul Nixon and Proofed.co.uk
Icon design by Aldo Cersal

www.multiplicit.com

The body text in this book is written in ITC Cheltenham Light. Headings are written in Open Sans Std and SemiBold.

Public domain flag images from flagpedia.net.

v1.02

Kind Words

Affiliate marketing is one of the most cost-effective and powerful ways for businesses to find their next customer, but it can be bewildering for advertisers, especially small businesses. That's why a book like this is worth its weight in gold. Helping SMEs navigate the industry with practical, hands-on insights about how to choose the right supplier, set commissions, choose the right affiliates as well as practical day to day tips, there are few manuals that offer such comprehensive guidance.
Michelle O'Sullivan, Global Customer Success Director – Awin Access

Steve expertly navigates through the fundamental concepts of affiliate marketing whilst providing practical guidance for affiliate marketers that's easily implemented. The tips, challenges and suggestions presented in this book make it a must read for all new business owners, marketers and account managers wanting to learn and master the art of affiliate marketing.
Seth Rubin, MD, Grow by Tradedoubler

"A really impressively detailed and comprehensive companion guide to anyone taking first steps into our industry
Richard Dennys, CEO, Webgains

"Even with ten years plus experience in affiliate marketing I have literally already found a use for your book. My team will definitely be using it. Great work!
Craig Mitchell, Head of Broadband and Mobile, Stickee

Steve has been in the partnerships industry for a long time and what he doesn't know probably isn't worth knowing. I found his instructional blog posts very useful, so it's fantastic to have all of that brought together and greatly expanded upon in this book. A great resource for anyone new to affiliate management or just looking to brush up on their knowledge.

John Coulson Partnerships Consultant

"At MVF we work with many publishers, partners and advertisers and everyone benefits when they have good advice and support from the industry. This book will especially help new advertisers make informed decisions and create profitable partnerships.

Tom Morgan, Co-Founder, MVF

A valuable resource, easy to understand and a great insight into an industry that may appear complex at first but is actually pretty simple when you know how. Steve's in-depth knowledge and straight to the point style make this a guide to go back to again and again.

Anne Watson, Director of Partnerships, Northern Europe, Webloyalty

People who are new to affiliate marketing would do well to read this cover to cover before staring their new job. So many colours to the affiliate rainbow, with diversification never seeming to stop; but a very good foundation stone can be found in this manuscript. There are even a few surprises for us veterans.

Matthew Rand, Affiliate Account Manager, Reader's Digest

Steve's detailed advice should be considered indispensable for anyone looking to kickstart their affiliate activity, new affiliate managers and even established merchants looking for the latest in best practice advice.

Louis Sabet, Managing Director, Bigupdata

Preface

“Affiliate marketing is one of the most democratic types of online advertising. Anyone can be an affiliate publisher, and a thriving global community of marketers promote anything from fashion to gaming to financial services to homeware. An exciting new development has recently extended the open philosophy of affiliate marketing to the advertisers whose products and services are being promoted.

This aspect of the industry is so new that there isn't a universal name for this new way to enter the affiliate industry. I have loosely dubbed them 'self-managed' programs, but other perfectly valid names could be 'entry-level', 'self-service' or 'easy access'.

Regardless of what you call them, what they all have in common is that they make affiliate marketing possible for thousands of small to medium enterprises earlier in their development.

A typical self-managed program is easy to set up, cost effective to operate, and does not come with a long-term commitment. By removing the obvious 'pain points' the affiliate industry has unlocked a potent tool for thousands upon thousands of new advertisers.

While the costs are manageable, the responsibilities and work required to succeed are the same as any affiliate program. Arguably, these programs often need more time and effort to flourish.

With 20 years of experience in affiliate marketing and over a decade of helping advertisers launch affiliate programs, I knew I could help newcomers to the industry navigate those tricky first steps.

First came a series of blog posts, and then this book. I approached three well-respected European affiliate networks and was delighted when they jumped at the chance to contribute.

This book was written for any small or medium-sized business that has recently launched an affiliate program or is thinking of setting one up. While it pays specific attention to the new generation of accessible programs offered by the likes of Awin, Tradedoubler and Webgains, I have tried to include enough tips and advice to help anyone managing an affiliate program 'in house'.

I hope this guide will equip SMEs and new program managers with usable and practical advice about the challenges and opportunities that new affiliate programs face. The advice should help you to navigate the tricky first stages of running an affiliate program and establish affiliate marketing as a permanent and effective marketing tool for your business.

Steve Lownds

Contents

1: Foreword

Seth Rubin

Managing Director – Grow by Tradedoubler

"The affiliate industry is blessed with some of the greatest digital marketing minds, who continuously innovate to provide their advertisers with access to new audiences. Affiliate marketing is not just another digital channel but rather a melting pot of invention, opportunities, and ideas, deployed across multiple channels. In fact, the landscape is so diverse that nearly all online experiences are influenced, in some way or another, by affiliate marketing.

Like Steve, I have been fortunate enough to experience wholesale changes in the industry. From the early days, where bedroom affiliates reigned supreme, through the ecommerce and mobile booms, to today; where the largest affiliates are now household names and social influencers can change the fortunes of a brand overnight.

Over the last two decades affiliate marketing has developed into a global industry worth billions of dollars and one that is essential for all retailers, big and small. This success, though, has raised the barriers for new businesses, especially when you look at the main networks who typically require clients to sign lengthy contracts, with costly set-up and ongoing fees. Whilst publishers often only want to work with larger brands. These obstacles meant that smaller businesses were mostly unable to participate...until now.

Since launching Grow in June 2020, Tradedoubler has welcomed thousands of new businesses and smaller advertisers, who were looking for a risk-free way to build their affiliate programs, earlier in their online journey.

Low costs, short-term contracts, and new technology, coupled with assurances from a diverse range of affiliates provides the perfect blend of ingredients that new advertisers need to become successful.

Everyone involved in facilitating this opportunity – the networks in this book, the affiliates working with new brands, and industry professionals, like Steve, want to see new businesses utilise and benefit from affiliate marketing.

If you are about to start your own affiliate program, then this book is a must read. It's an ideal primer and a great reference that will help you get to grips with this fascinating industry. The book makes, often complicated, concepts seem simple and clarifies terminology unique to the space so that you can get up to speed quickly.

Steve's expert knowledge and wealth of experience shines throughout this book; his tips are spot-on and suggestions, very relevant – whether you're a start-up or an already successful business. He clearly guides you through the detail, to get you started, launch your first program, and select the right affiliates to work with, setting you up for long-lasting success.

And don't forget, a self-managed program gives you a unique opportunity to grow your business by employing an army of brilliant marketeers, who utilise a variety of channels to drive sales for you. Afterall, you are the best advocate for your business, and best placed to make agile and informed decisions that will help you work smarter, react quicker and ultimately unlock a whole new world of opportunities.

You have taken the first step, in reading this book. Good luck on your journey.

Seth Rubin

2: How this book is organised

Chapters and sections

The book is organised into chapters and sections.

Chapters cover a specific aspect of building an affiliate program, such as 'Recruitment' or 'Account management'.

Sections address a specific task or topic, such as 'How affiliate tracking works' or 'Product feeds'.

Goals

Each chapter or section is introduced with a quick explanation of what it is trying to achieve.

Responsibilities

When a section introduces a task or concept that is integral to managing your program, it is introduced as a 'new responsibility'.

New responsibility

'Validate' your sales regularly to ensure affiliates receive their commission as quickly as possible.

Assumptions

This book is designed to accompany you through the various stages of planning and implementing your affiliate program. Each chapter begins with an explanation of where you are assumed to be in the process.

Safety and security

Some topics and techniques covered in this book require extra measures to protect your business and affiliates from unintended outcomes. Where necessary, these steps are discussed under 'safety and security'.

Top tips

The book is sprinkled with short ideas and tips to help make individual tasks easier.

Top tip
Pay attention to the top tips - they could make your life easier!

Other considerations

Program' vs 'Programme'

This book is written in British English with one exception; it adopts the American spelling of the word 'program', since that is more widely used in the affiliate industry. You are free to use either spelling – in your own communications.

Currency

All examples are in Euros. Don't worry if this is not your local currency – the examples in this book apply to any currency or region.

Networks

Tables comparing network features are in alphabetic order for easy reference. Other mentions are randomised for fairness.

3: Introduction

Before you start to plan and build your affiliate program, you should know what you are getting into. Here is a very brief overview of affiliate marketing and how it works.

Goals for this chapter

By the end of this chapter, you should understand how affiliate marketing works and be comfortable with the terms used throughout this book.

This chapter will cover:

Assumptions

This chapter will assume you are starting your affiliate marketing journey. You have heard about the tremendous potential of self-managed affiliate programs, but you would like to understand more about the affiliate industry and what it can do for you.

3.1 Common terms

The affiliate industry is full of acronyms and abbreviations. Here are a few that will help you get the most out of this guide.

Merchant/advertiser

The merchant operates the affiliate program, rewarding affiliates with a commission payment when they generate sales. The terms **merchant** and **advertiser** are used interchangeably throughout this book and the affiliate industry.

Affiliate/publisher

Affiliates own the websites, email lists or apps that drive traffic to your affiliate program. They are rewarded with commissions when they generate a sale. The terms **affiliate** and **publisher** are used interchangeably throughout this book and the affiliate industry.

Network

The **affiliate network**, or simply **the network**, is a third party that helps power your affiliate program. Their technology provides tracking, reporting and payments. Three networks are featured in this book; Awin, Tradedoubler and Webgains - are networks.

Program

The term 'program' is the scheme that the publisher enrols in to promote an advertiser. It is a blanket term that describes the terms, resources and processes that drive the relationship between the network, advertiser and publisher.

Self-managed program

A **self-managed program** is a specific type of program offered by affiliate networks. It combines an accessible payment structure and simplified features to make affiliate marketing accessible and rewarding for small to medium-sized businesses.

The key distinguishing feature is that the advertiser is directly responsible for administering and promoting the program, unlike more traditional programs where the network and/or other agencies bear some of the responsibility for performance.

Commission

The **commission** is the reward paid to affiliates for generating a valid sale or lead.

CPA

This represents two different abbreviations with three possible meanings:

1. Cost Per Action (payment model) - Paying a commission when a visitor completes a specific action on your website.
2. Cost Per Acquisition (payment model) - Similar to the above, but some people call it acquisition because you are acquiring a customer
3. **Cost Per Acquisition** (commission) - The cost paid for an acquisition, basically the commission. Affiliates often ask 'What is the CPA?' meaning 'What will we be paid?' ***This is the definition we will use throughout this book.***

SEO

Search Engine Optimisation. Some affiliates rely solely on SEO to attract new visitors, while others supplement it with other promotion methods. Traffic from SEO is called 'organic' traffic.

Organic traffic

Website traffic which is obtained via **non-paid** methods, usually search engines such as Google, Yahoo, or Bing.

Organic traffic is desirable because typically you don't have to pay for it.

Channel

A way to differentiate different types of marketing activity. Paid media, affiliate marketing and Direct marketing are all considered distinct digital marketing 'channels'.

By separating marketing activity and results into channels, marketers can compare and understand the results and benefits.

PPC/CPC

Pay-Per-Click, or Cost-Per-Click, is a type of digital advertising in which advertisers pay a fee each time one of their advertisements is clicked. You only pay when a visitor clicks your ad, so it is essentially a method of 'buying' visits to your website. The most popular PPC platform is Google Ads, previously known as Google AdWords.

ROI

Return on Investment. The amount of income or revenue lost or gained from marketing activity. A high ROI means the marketing activity was worthwhile, while a low or negative ROI usually indicates it was not successful.

ROAS

Return on Ad Spend. ROAS is a popular way to express Return on Investment commonly used in digital marketing.

3.2 What is affiliate marketing?

Affiliate marketing is a type of digital marketing in which website owners are rewarded when they deliver a specific result - usually a paying customer.

Affiliates or **publishers** earn money by promoting products or services. They are only rewarded when they generate a specific outcome for the advertiser, usually an e-commerce sale.

The **merchant** or **advertiser** sells the product being promoted. This book was written to help new advertisers launch and run an affiliate program, so it is likely **you** are the advertiser.

Publishers promote a product or service **for free**. The advertiser rewards the publisher with a commission when a sale is made.

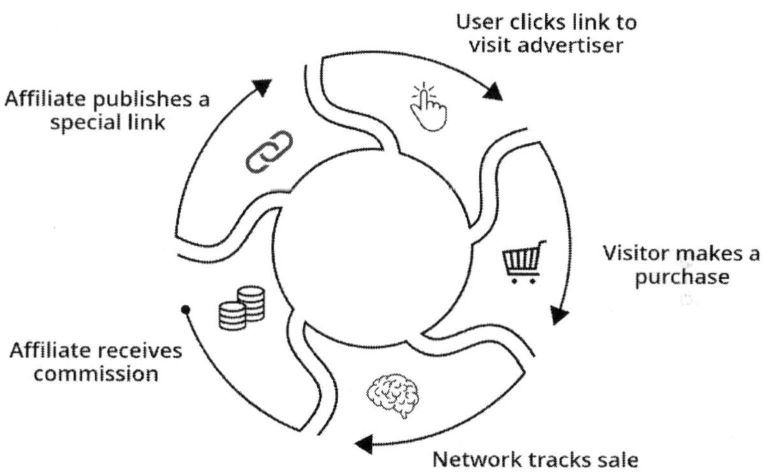

An affiliate program is a win-win relationship between publishers and advertisers. Since publishers are only paid when they generate a sale or lead, the amount they earn is directly linked to how well they perform.

Successful publishers can repeat this simple process hundreds or even thousands of times a day.

Affiliate marketing is responsible for tens of thousands of such transactions every minute of every day, across a diverse range of products, services and industries.

Once several affiliate partners start referring quality traffic several partners on board it is probable that there will be several potential customers progressing through the purchasing journey at any time

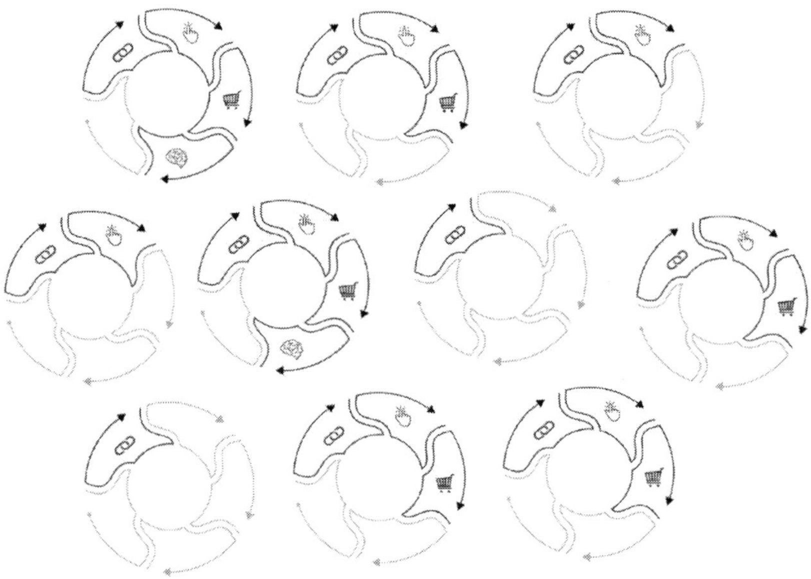

Affiliate managers encourage partners to drive new, and also to increase the chance that each consumer who clicks an affiliate link will complete the transaction.

The advertiser receives something they value – a paying customer, and the affiliate is rewarded with a commission.

The goal of this book

This book was written for any small or medium-sized business that has recently launched an affiliate program or is thinking of setting one up.

It shares tips and advice to help you launch and get the most out of a new affiliate program.

The affiliate industry created self-managed programs to introduce you to this exciting form of digital marketing and help you decide whether it works for your business.

The goal of this book is to help you make that decision. Is affiliate marketing right for you, and can it safely and reliably help you meet your business goals?

The guides, advice and sample policies in this book should help you to plan and launch an affiliate program and engage with a wide range of affiliate publishers.

For everyone who contributed to this book, 'success' will be when you **outgrow** the 'self-managed' or 'entry-level' label, and affiliate marketing becomes a key part of your digital marketing strategy.

3.3 Meet the key players

Who makes up the affiliate relationship? What are their goals, and what role do they play in making your program successful?

The advertiser

The advertiser, or merchant, is in charge of the affiliate program and the products it promotes. Since this is a book about affiliate management, that is probably you.

Your job is to shape your affiliate program into a genuine opportunity for your affiliates and your own business. You provide the structure required to make everything work and the inspiration and encouragement that encourages affiliates to work on your behalf.

Your affiliates

Affiliates or publishers come in all shapes and sizes. Some of the largest companies in the world are also affiliates, while others work alone. These can be bloggers, vloggers, website owners or media buyers. Many publishers nowadays don't even have websites, but they all have one thing in common - they want your program to be a success so they can earn commission from promoting it.

Affiliates earn a commission by promoting a product or service made by another retailer or advertiser. They only receive a commission after the action you are looking for has occurred - a shipped order or genuine lead.

The affiliate's job is to generate traffic that they believe will help you achieve your goals.

The affiliate network

The network is the bridge between the affiliate and the merchant. Its technology makes your relationship possible by allowing you to track sales and by making payments seamless and easy.

The network's job is to make your relationship with affiliates as smooth as possible and to protect your business by providing technology and services that are modern, reliable and legally compliant. Good networks actively work to encourage new relationships through new innovations and regular communication with all their affiliates.

The consumer/customer

Let's not forget the customer who ultimately purchases your product. Affiliate marketing can have a massive impact on their shopping experience.

Affiliate marketing can enrich their shopping journey by introducing them to new products, helping them find better prices or introducing unique benefits for loyalty.

The consumer doesn't have a job to do like the other players mentioned above, but they are no less important. Keeping the customer in mind will ensure your affiliate program is a genuine opportunity for everyone involved.

3.4 Self-managed affiliate programs

What is special about 'self-managed' programs?

Affiliate marketing is powerful and effective because it rewards **results**. However, the barrier to entry can be quite high, with long term contracts and high access fees.

Self-managed programs were born out of a desire to make the affiliate industry more accessible. Since early 2020, several networks have launched self-managed programs to help SMEs access those results at an earlier stage in their development.

It is the fastest-growing segment of the affiliate industry, with thousands of new programs launching every year. Accessible contracts and simplified requirements mean almost any online business can launch a new affiliate program quickly and cost-effectively.

Self-managed programs usually share a few distinguishing features:

- 'Self-service' account management
- Low monthly cost
- Industry-standard override fees (usually 30%)
- Quick launch process
- Curated or restricted feature set
- Short minimum commitment

Will my self-managed program be taken seriously?

While there may be a few minor technical differences, self-managed advertisers have access to all the same tools and opportunities as the rest of the industry.

Since 2020, thousands of new advertisers have taken advantage of self-managed terms to launch new affiliate programs. There is no reason why a self-managed affiliate program can't be as successful as any other affiliate program.

Do I have to use a network?

Affiliate networks act as the link between retailers and the affiliates that promote them.

Any advertiser can build and power their own affiliate program, but networks add a lot of value. They provide proven tracking technology, host your creatives and other resources and coordinate payments to your affiliate partners. The most important thing they offer is an ecosystem of affiliates ready for you to recruit.

In-house affiliate programs must work hard to build the affiliate's confidence in the tracking and payment processes, something networks have already done.

Which networks are featured in this book?

This book includes examples and comparisons for three self-managed offerings: **Webgains Edge**, **Grow by Tradedoubler** and **Awin Access**.

The three networks chosen to be featured in this book were selected because:

- They have a dedicated self-managed offering
- They have been active for several years
- Their service is available across Europe and beyond
- Their networks are open to legitimate publishers of any size

Awin Access

Awin Access launched in 2020, increasing the reach kick-starting a whole new area of growth for the affiliate industry.

In their own words

"The IAB's PoweringUp research found 40% of SMEs do not use digital marketing tactics and lack the knowledge and confidence to do so.

They have also been underserved by the affiliate industry and so we spoke to them about what they needed to run a successful affiliate program. They told us any solution has to be as automated as possible, easy to use and low risk.

So firstly we streamlined the sign up and integration process. Awin Access has a simple application form as well as plugins to all the major e-commerce platforms such as Shopify and WooCommerce.

We then give small businesses the ability to test the channel with no sign-up fees and one month free on a low risk, 90-day commitment. After that they're free to walk away by giving 14 days' notice at any time if affiliate marketing is not right for them.

We are confident that our user interface is intuitive and easy to use, however, we regularly provide our Awin Access customers with online guides, video content and de-jargonised webinars.

The Access team is on hand to answer any enquiries and we offer help via live chat. We also offer new, daily partner recommendations drawn from our active pool of nearly half a million publishers.

Every Awin Access customer who opts in to hear from us also receives a series of emails from day one that walk through the essentials and how to get the most out of their affiliate program. These emails also introduce our Access customers to new publisher and partner opportunities, including technology solutions that help optimise their on-site click to sale conversion rates.

What's more, Awin Access doesn't just appeal to individual businesses. Incubators, accelerators, agencies and small business organisations such as the Federation of Small Businesses have also been keen adopters. Olivia Martyn from Founders Factory commented, "Awin is helping our start-ups to build great affiliate partnerships".

Since Awin Access officially launched in 2020, more than 3,200 advertisers have launched a program on the solution and around two new brands begin their Awin journey with us every working day of the year. Start your affiliate journey with us today.

Awin Access is available in:

- United Kingdom
- United States
- Germany
- Belgium
- Austria
- Switzerland
- Finland
- Spain
- Portugal
- Eastern Europe
- Ireland
- France
- Italy
- Poland
- Sweden
- Denmark
- The Netherlands
- Norway
- Brazil

Grow by Tradedoubler

Grow launched in 2020, offering easy integration, ready-to-launch partners and easy access to a range of digital marketing channels.

In their own words

"Tradedoubler, the industry's longest standing affiliate network (since 1999), launched Grow in mid-2020 with the aim to make affiliate marketing smart, simple and accessible.

Grow is the only solution that allows you to sign-up online, and in your own time. We pride ourselves on simplicity and automation which doesn't stop when you join.

Our range of applications, available for the leading ecommerce platforms enables our clients to launch their programs themselves, within just 10 minutes of joining. Once you've signed up, simply login to your store's management console and download our app which will help you configure your tracking code and manage all your technical requirements out-the-box.

Our app provides you with a beautiful dashboard, allowing you to see your performance stats inside your store's management console. It also creates the perfect product feed for your affiliates to use and pulls your discount codes automatically, ensuring your affiliates have all they need to promote your business.

The platform is purpose built for the self-service sector, with automation and simplicity at its core. Inside you'll find the tools needed to run your program. Some of our unique features include instant messaging with your affiliates, credit card billing and a comprehensive knowledge base.

With no set-up or joining fees and the first 30-days free, Grow is the perfect place to start your affiliate journey. Grow has no minimum commitment, simply give 30-days' notice, should you wish to leave.

We offer a free introductory call and promote your business to our network of more than 180,000 affiliates too, to get you started. Your Grow team offers ongoing training and support, and send regular newsletters that include recommendations, tips, and access to the most lucrative opportunities in your market.

Grow has helped more than 3,500 clients, from the EU, US, UK, and Australia launch their affiliate programs, with more than 200 new clients joining each month.

GROW your business with us, join today!

Grow by Tradedoubler is available in:

- United Kingdom
- United States
- New Zealand
- Germany
- Austria
- Switzerland
- Belgium
- Finland
- Spain
- Central Eastern Europe
- Mexico
- Ireland
- France
- Australia
- Italy
- Poland
- Sweden
- Denmark
- The Netherlands
- Norway
- Portugal

Webgains Edge

Webgains Edge was launched in 2021 to offer almost unrestricted access to the Webgains platform at an affordable price.

In their own words

“ Webgains is one of the top global affiliate networks combining an intelligence lead platform and first-class service to drive online success for your business. With over 17 years' experience in the industry, we pride ourselves on our service above all. Whether you are a small emerging brand looking for that initial introduction into the Affiliate space to drive additional incremental revenue, or you are an established brand wanting to gain a competitive advantage - we have a bespoke solution for you.

Webgains Edge is an affiliate marketing service specifically tailored for small-to-medium sized businesses who are searching for additional cost-effective revenue streams.

Edge provides a simple and affordable solution to running an affiliate program and partnering with the biggest affiliates across the UK, EU, US and Australia.

- When you sign up to Webgains Edge, you will be assisted by our launch team to ensure your affiliate tracking is installed correctly on your site and that your program is primed for success.
- Once your program is live, we will provide you with ongoing training and support.
- Fast response, high-quality customer service delivered by our team of experts.
- Unique AI-driven recommendations from our network of 250,000 affiliates.
- Easy-to-use technical platform.
- Exclusive Webgains Academy training.

- Weekly newsletters with affiliate opportunities and recommendations.
- On average a Webgains Edge Client generates over €35,000 in sales during the first six months of their program.
- Unlimited use of the full Webgains suite including publisher discovery and dynamic commissioning tools
- 48-hour client support response time (within standard working hours)

Over 1,800 businesses profit from the services of Webgains to deliver online sales worldwide. By investing in talent and technology, multi-award winning Webgains has created the optimum blend of human and artificial intelligence. Webgains' Machine Learning Technology includes features such as Affiliate Discovery, Product Discovery and Smart Commissioning, to make smarter connections for advertisers and affiliates alike.

Webgains Edge is available in:

United Kingdom	Canada
United States	Spain
Australia	Italy
Ireland	Poland
Germany	Sweden
France	Denmark
Austria	Finland
Switzerland	Norway
The Netherlands	

4: Fundamentals

Affiliate managements starts with the affiliate manager. Let's talk about the roles and responsibilities of an affiliate manager, and what the role entails.

Goals for this chapter

This section discusses two indispensable components in a successful affiliate program; the tracking technology and you, the affiliate manager.

This chapter will cover:

Assumptions

It is Day 1. You are ready to start the rewarding and exciting process or creating and managing a new affiliate program.

4.1 Self-service

It is very important to remember that 'self-managed' programs are designed to be run without regular intervention by the network.

That does not mean you are left with no support at all, but it does mean you are responsible for the 'account managing' your affiliate partners and the overall performance of your program.

While self-managed programs are designed to be easy to set up and have a short contract commitment, the time and effort required to make it successful is significant.

You **can** still ask your network for assistance for technical and compliance questions, and they all make a range of online resources available to advise and guide you.

Here is some of the support that is typically available:

- Pre/post launch consultations
- Technical support via email
- Dedicated training material
- Live chat (working hours)
- Training webinars
- YouTube Tutorials
- Advertiser hub / support area
- Wiki / knowledge base for technical information
- Publisher' recruitment suggestions
- Bookable phone consultations

Top tip

Self-service makes it the responsibility of you the advertiser to drive performance. Look at this as an opportunity - with less middle-men between you and your publishers decisions can be made much more quickly.

4.2 Accessing support from your network

Most self-managed affiliate programs are **self-service**. While you won't receive personalised support, the network is still available to assist you with technical, payment or service-related issues.

The starting point to receive support is usually your advertiser control panel. The 'help' or 'support' chapter should contain instructions on how to contact your network and receive support.

New responsibility
Research and understand the various options and support routes available for your self-managed program

AWIN

Standard support is offered via email and live chat, both accessible through your advertiser interface. In addition, Awin Access clients have access to the following resources:

- Monthly pdf performance reports
- Interface training webinar
- Webinar Centre for Small Businesses
- YouTube Tutorials
- Advertiser Success Centre
- Central support team email
- Real-time live chat within working hours
- Extensive technical wiki

Standard support is provided via email and bookable phone calls, both accessible through your advertiser interface. In addition, Webgains Edge clients have access to the following resources:

- Unlimited use of the full Webgains suite including publisher discovery and dynamic commissioning tools
- 48-hour client support response time (within standard working hours)
- Email support from a dedicated team
- Dedicated training material
- 'Top publisher' recruitment suggestions
- Platform walkthrough videos
- Bookable training calls
- Webgains Academy

Standard support is provided via email and bookable phone calls, both accessible through your advertiser interface. In addition, Grow by Tradedoubler clients have access to the following resources:

- Dedicated support for Grow clients
- Bookable calls with local representatives
- Top-performing recommended partners
- Dedicated blog
- Comprehensive knowledge base

Top tip

Your network will help out with important technical or payment-related issues, but the performance and success of your new affiliate program are entirely your responsibility.

4.3 What do affiliate managers do?

The affiliate manager is the main point of contact for an affiliate program. They recruit new partners, manage existing relationships and actively work to improve the performance of the affiliate marketing channel.

What does it involve?

The affiliate managers role is to **take responsibility** for the performance and improvement of the affiliate channel.

Each of these tasks is discussed in detail in later chapters, but some of the routine activities for an affiliate manager are:

- Recruiting new affiliate partners
- Convincing new affiliates to actively promote the brand
- Encouraging active affiliates to refer more new customers
- Optimising the program and website to help affiliates get the best results
- Listening to and acting upon feedback from the business about affiliates, even if it is uncomfortable
- Listening to and acting upon feedback from affiliates about your business, even if it is uncomfortable
- Reporting on the affiliate channels performance
- Advocating the involvement of affiliates to the wider business
- Negotiating extra coverage
- Negotiating bespoke commission rates

The most important role the affiliate manager performs is as an advocate for both sides of the affiliate relationship.

As the key point of contact for affiliate partners it is the affiliate managers role to represent and promote their interests to the wider business, while making sure affiliates are always aware of the advertisers strengths and priorities.

Is it a full-time job?

You can certainly spend all day managing an affiliate program, but the affiliate manager for a self-managed program is likely to hold a range of responsibilities.

That's ok - the role can scale with the size of your program and business.

If possible, nominate one person to act as a "focus" for the affiliate program. Affiliate publishers respond well to a consistent point of contact, and it ensures important information is not overlooked by different team members.

What skills do affiliate managers need?

Anyone can be an affiliate manager regardless of their skill set, but a few basic things help:

- Basic HTML/CSS
- Good literacy and the ability to write persuasive communications
- Basic Excel skills

4.4 How affiliate tracking works

Tracking technology is integral to the affiliate industry. Without advanced, robust tracking the affiliate industry would not be able to track millions of transactions per day.

Goals for this section
While you don't need to understand every technical detail, this section aims to equip you with a general understanding of the tracking process.

Standard cookie-based tracking

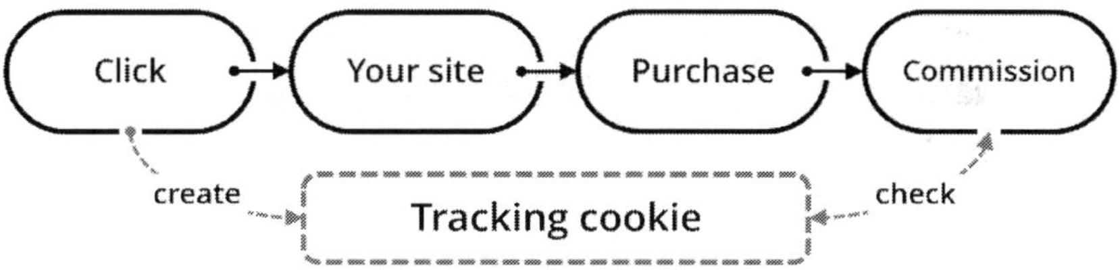

Affiliate tracking has evolved over the years, but the general concept has remained the same:

1. A visitor clicks an affiliate link
2. A tracking cookie is placed on the visitor's device
3. The visitor arrives on the merchant website
4. The visitor makes a purchase
5. The tracking script on the order confirmation page checks the customers device for a tracking cookie
6. If a valid cookie is found, the sale tracks in the network platform

Throughout this book, we will use standard industry terms to describe the tracking process. Affiliate tracking placed on a consumer's device will be called the **affiliate cookie**, regardless of the actual technology used. The tracking installed on your website will be called the **tracking script**.

Common tracking terms

Last click wins

Last click wins means the affiliate commission is awarded to the affiliate that created the most recent tracking cookie on the customer's device.

This method of attributing sales to marketing channels is the default for the affiliate industry because:

- It is easy to understand
- It extends the window during which an affiliate sale can track, thus generating more overrides for the network

Cookie duration

The **cookie duration** defines how long the tracking cookie stays in the customer's browser after their original click. The longer this window lasts, the better the affiliate's chance of generating a commission.

Every time a visitor clicks an affiliate link the cookie duration is reset and the countdown starts again.

Affiliate networks make it easy to change the cookie duration, but most self-managed programs don't include this option. Don't be concerned about this; your network will have chosen a reasonable and fair default period.

Assisted sales

The last click wins model is the only real choice for the overall affiliate industry, but some affiliate or product types need a different approach.

This is where **assisted sales** come into play, helping you to reward influencers when they contributed to a sale but didn't refer the important final click.

Assisted sales are not required for every program, but in industries with a lot of influencers and content affiliates, they play an important role in partnership marketing.

Bloggers and influencers are good examples because they can generate a lot of interest and awareness for a product, but the consumer may go on to purchase through another affiliate - perhaps a cashback or voucher website.

First vs third party cookies

A cookie is simply a small text file that is created by your web browser. It is an easy and convenient way for websites to store long term information.

Cookies can only be accessed by the website which created them. Your website cannot 'read' a cookie created by the affiliate network, and vice-versa.

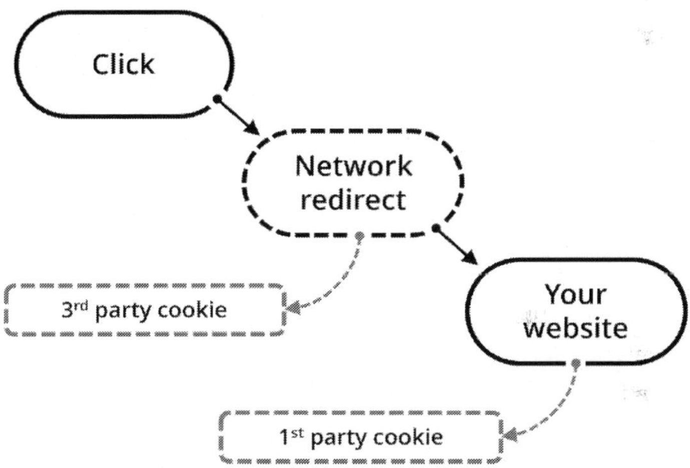

If the cookie is created by your affiliate network, it is a **third party** cookie.

If the cookie is created by your own website it is a **first party** cookie.

While traditional affiliate cookies are created by the network when the visitor clicks a link, **first-party cookies** originate from your own website. That makes them much harder for browsers and security software to block.

First party tracking is the first stage of an advanced tracking solution, and most networks now offer a first-party tracking solution as standard.

First party cookies often require a 'master' or 'container' tag to be placed on every page of your website. The tracking plug-in or installation instructions for your ecommerce platform should take care of this.

First Party cookies are the default option for a modern affiliate program, but they do still have some weaknesses:

- Some security software may still block them
- E-commerce software with lots of internal redirects can prevent a first party cookie being created
- 'private' or 'incognito' browser sessions discard cookies after you close the browser
- First time visitors to your website may be required to accept the cookie policy before you are permitted to create first party cookies.

Container tags

Your network may ask you to install a 'container tag' on every page of your website. This is a universal toolkit of useful functions that help sales track. They are also known as 'master' or 'universal' tags.

Container tags perform the following functions:

- Create 'first party' cookies for all affiliate traffic
- Enable 'cross-device' tracking
- Allow easy installation of approved technology providers (see section 9.18: Technology partners)

Most official tracking plug-ins install the container tag automatically, but if you have to install the tracking manually the installation instructions guide you through the process.

Other types of tracking

In the early days of affiliate marketing's popularity, there was only one main way to get online: a desktop computer. Nowadays, people can access the Internet from laptops, tablets, phones and even cars.

Attitudes to online security and tracking have also changed, and web browsers and security software often block the humble tracking cookie. Old-fashioned third-party cookies alone are no longer sufficient for advertisers' needs. However, the networks are always working to keep up with the times.

Cross-device tracking

Sometimes consumers might research a purchase on one device and complete the purchase on another. In dealing with this, **cross-device tracking** attempts to remember consumers when they use a different device. Each network implements cross-device tracking differently.

Cookie-free tracking

Modern browsers and programming languages offer opportunities for novel tracking methods that don't use cookies. These include HTML5 storage and advanced device fingerprinting.

Server-to-server tracking

Server-to-server tracking is a way to track sales without relying on a user's web browser or any client-side technology. It is less likely to be blocked by security or ad-blocking software and is generally viewed as the most reliable tracking tool.

Server to server tracking is the best way to tell your network about a sale, but it doesn't know which sales should track and which ones shouldn't. It goes hand in hand with first party cookies to identify which sales came from affiliates and should receive commission.

How reliable is affiliate tracking?

As a rule, affiliate tracking is stable and reliable, but it is possible for some sales to be overlooked. Here are the most common reasons.

Caused by the publisher:

- The affiliate forgot to add the correct tracking to their links
- The tracking link became malformed or corrupted
- The affiliate is linking to an out-of-stock product. Sales will out-of-stock track, but the user experience and conversion rate will be negatively affected

Caused by the advertiser:

- The tracking script was accidentally removed from the e-commerce website
- The 'container' or 'master' tag was not present on the page the customer landed on, so the first party tracking cookie was not created
- The sale was attributed to another channel, such as PPC
- The attribution system is not recording affiliate traffic properly
- The customer landed on a page that immediately redirected them to another page, causing the website to 'forget' the visitor came from an affiliate.

Caused by the customer:

- The customer has installed software or a browser plug-in designed to block ads and online tracking
- The customer uses a web browser with built-in privacy features or tracking prevention
- The customer did not click an affiliate link

4.5 Order statuses

Every transaction has a 'status' that dictates whether the affiliate will receive a commission.

Goals for this section

After completing this section, you should understand the different statuses an order can pass through before commission is awarded to the affiliate.

The whole point of affiliate marketing is to only reward publishers when they deliver an action that is valuable for your business. For most standard affiliate programs that is usually a genuine sale or order.

To make sure you only reward the correct transactions, every order is assigned a status which changes through the life of the order.

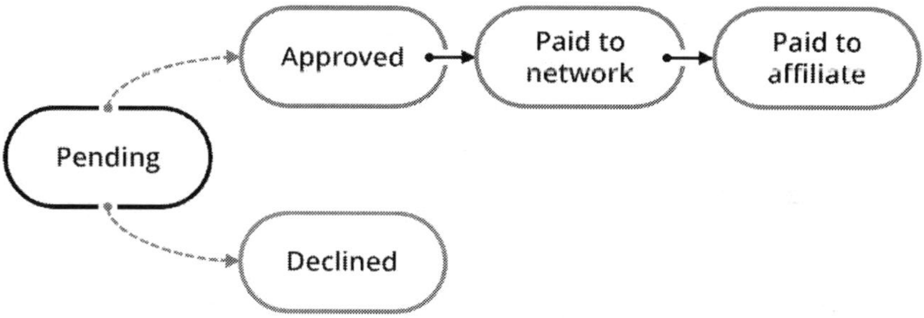

The following are the three most common and important statuses for orders:

Pending

An order which has recently tracked and is still waiting to be validated is classed as **pending**.

This is a *transient* status - it will eventually change to 'confirmed' or 'declined'.

Confirmed

A **confirmed** order is eligible to receive commission and can no longer be returned or cancelled. Once you are sure these criteria are met you can release the commission to the affiliate by confirming or approving it.

This is a *final* status - once a transaction is confirmed, it is unlikely to change again.

Declined

An order that is not eligible for commission is **declined**. The most common reasons for this are:

- The order did not ship
- The order was cancelled by the customer
- The order was returned by the customer

This is a *final* status - once a commission is declined, it is unlikely to change again.

Payment status

In addition to the validation status, every confirmed transaction also has a payment status. This tells you whether the affiliate has received the commission.

These statuses reflect whether you have paid the network and whether the funds have been passed to the affiliate.

There are three possible combinations:

- Awaiting payment to network
- Paid to network, not paid to affiliate
- Paid to affiliate

5: Costs and goals

Affiliate marketing is known as a cost-effective way to promote your business. The unique pay-for-performance model means the more you pay, the more sales you make for your business.

Goals for this chapter

By the end of this chapter, you should understand how affiliate networks charge for their service, how to set performance goals for your affiliate program and how to conduct fundamental performance-tracking calculations.

This chapter will cover:

Assumptions

This chapter assumes you are at the first stage of launching your affiliate program. Once you understand the costs, you are ready to start building your proposition and completing your online profile.

5.1 Costs

Affiliate networks charge you for their services using one of two mechanisms: monthly fees and overrides. It is important to understand the role these play in your total costs.

Goals for this section
This section aims to make sure you are comfortable with the concept of overrides and can understand the different elements that make up your affiliate program's total cost.

Two mechanisms are used to charge advertisers:

Monthly access fee

For self-managed programs, the **monthly access fee** is usually a nominal amount. The monthly charge doesn't generate profit for the network - its main purpose is to prove you are serious about your program and have the means to pay advertising fees.

Override

The **override** is calculated as a percentage of the commission you pay to affiliates. The standard override for self-managed programs is 30%.

The override is usually the main cost for self-managed programs. This model stays true to affiliate marketing's pay-per-performance ethos.

The cost is directly related to how many sales you make and the commission you pay, making it easy to predict and manage.

Calculating the override

For these examples, we will use the industry-standard 30% override, or a factor of 1.3.

If you pay €10 commission, a 30% override will increase your costs by €3:

```
€10 × 1.3 = €13
```

Don't forget VAT

Affiliate commissions and overrides are eligible for VAT. If your business is not VAT-registered, then the tax effectively increases your costs.

If your business cannot reclaim VAT, it may help to use an override value of 56%*.

```
  Commission = €10
+ Override: 30% of €10 = €3
+ VAT: 20% of €13 = €2.60
= €15.60
```

becomes...

```
  €10 + 56%
= €15.60
```

* Assuming 30% override and 20% VAT

Calculating the cost of an individual sale

The cost per sale is simply a product of the commission and override. This may not represent the final cost to your business, but it is a handy calculation to understand whether an individual transaction is within your means.

$$\text{Commission} + \text{Override} + \text{VAT (optional)} = \text{COST of Sale}$$

Understanding the total cost to your business

You can run this calculation monthly or weekly, including extra fees, to determine the total cost per sale.

This process yields the most useful information when you apply it to the same period as your fixed monthly fee. If a monthly fee covers the period 1st-31st July, then apply this formula to assess sales within the same time frame.

$$\frac{\text{Monthly fees (VAT optional)} + \text{Commissions (VAT optional)} + \text{Override (VAT optional)}}{\text{Number of sales}} = \text{Overall CPA}$$

The impact of fixed costs

The overall cost per sale changes with every sale when you take a monthly or fixed fee into account. When you present it on a graph, the effect is very pronounced at first but decreases with every subsequent sale.

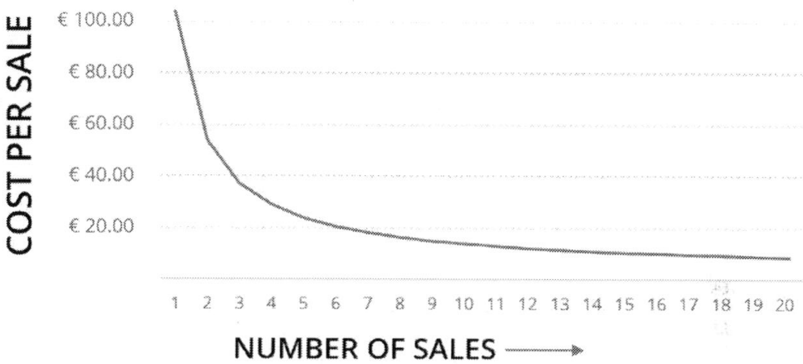

Based on: €100 monthly cost, €3 commission and 30% override

There will be a point at which the curve of the graph becomes less pronounced and affiliate marketing 'makes sense' financially. In the simple example above, that is around 10 sales per month.

In practical terms, this means your costs may appear very high during the first few days or weeks after launch when your program has not yet made very many sales.

New responsibility
Monitor the costs of your program to make sure you understand how much your affiliate sales cost your business.

5.2 ROAS

ROAS, or Return on Ad Spend, is a common measure of success in affiliate marketing. It helps you to understand how much a marketing channel contributes to your business.

Goals for this section
This section introduces a standard measure of success in digital marketing. After completing the examples below, you should be able to apply the same calculations to your own program.

There are several formulas used to calculate ROAS. This book will use the following method because the outcome is a percentage that is easy to understand.

$$\frac{\text{Revenue from affiliates}}{\text{Cost of advertising}} \times 100 = \text{ROAS}$$

The final part of the formula - multiplying the result by 100 - turns it into a percentage, which allows you to see exactly how much influence your affiliate commissions are having.

For example, if you spent €1,000 in commissions to generate €10,000 in sales, the calculation would be:

```
  €10,000 revenue
÷ [€1,000 commission + €300 override]
× 100
```

The answer for this example is **769%** - a very healthy ROAS.

Don't forget VAT

The cost includes the network override, but it is up to you whether to include VAT or other taxes. If your business is not VAT-registered, it may be prudent to consider the tax as an extra cost.

If you do include VAT, make sure you add it to every element – the commission *and* the override.

What is a good ROAS?

A reasonable ROAS depends on your industry, the cost of your products and your margins. However, a ROAS over 500% is generally considered worthwhile.

Remember -- **your ROAS can be too high**. For example, if your ROAS is 5000%, it could mean you are playing it too safe.

In this instance, you could consider trading some of your ROAS for new reach and growth by testing new partners or investing in tenancies to reach new audiences.

5.3 Self-managed cost structures

Every affiliate network has different fees and conditions, but the common denominator is the override.

Cost is just one factor to think about when you are choosing a network. Self-managed fee structures are designed to be manageable and affordable, so don't feel obliged only to consider the cheapest.

	AWIN	grow by Tradedoubler	WEBGAINS
Sign-up fee	No setup fee	No setup fee	No setup fee
Monthly cost (UK)	€75 (GBP)	€44.99	
Monthly cost (EUR)	€75	€49.99	
Override	30%	30%	30%
Minimum monthly spend			€200 or €200
Auto-validation	Variable	Variable	Variable
Commission groups	1	1	Unlimited
Exclusivity?	Yes	Yes	Yes
Minimum contract	3 months	3 months	3 months
Payment methods	Direct debit	Direct debit	Direct debit, Bank transfer Debit/credit card

These prices and terms were correct at the time of writing, but could change at any time; the self-managed landscape is developing fast, and it is likely that the networks listed will launch new ways to charge and add value for their clients over the coming months and years.

5.4 Setting your goals

Before we discuss building your proposition, ask yourself: what do you want out of your new affiliate program?

Goals for this section
This section will encourage you to think about what you want to achieve with your affiliate program. The more defined your goals, the easier it will be to achieve them.

General goals

It is important to have an overall aim for your program. With this in place, any time you aren't sure about a decision, you can always ask yourself, 'will it help achieve my goal?'

'Make loads of money' is a perfectly valid goal for your business, but it isn't the only one. A lot of successful affiliate programs never make a profit from affiliate sales, but they still contribute to the business in different ways.

These are common priorities for an affiliate program:

- Increase revenue (sales)
- Increase market share
- Hit volume targets for a specific product or service
- Hit a specific sales target
- Build the brand and get the word out
- Attract repeat customers

All of the above?

Maybe you want everything - new customers, increased revenue, more market share, the works!

That is understandable. All the goals listed above involve a positive contribution to your business, so why not ask for everything?

Prioritising one or two key goals doesn't mean you have to neglect the others; it just helps you organise your efforts and simplifies the task ahead of you. Look at the list a different way: try putting the goals in priority order - which one is the *most important* to your business?

At least one of your goals should include a number that can be measured.

The most common measures of success are:

- Revenue
- Order volume
- ROAS

To get you started, here are a couple of sensible recommendations:

- Measure your affiliates' progress by keeping track of the **revenue** and **total orders** that each affiliate generates
- Monitor **ROAS** and **total orders** to understand how effective and sustainable your program is

5.5 Should I pay on a CPS or CPL basis?

Before you start thinking about commission levels, you need to decide exactly *what* action to reward affiliates for. The payment model defines exactly what triggers a commission for your affiliates.

Goals for this section
After completing this section, you should be able to decide which payment model is best suited to your program - CPS or CPL.

There are dozens of ways to calculate and pay commission, but we will concentrate on the two most common: CPS and CPL.

This chapter will look at the differences and help you to ensure you choose the right one.

In a nutshell

Whichever model you choose, your affiliate program should **reward the action that your business values**.

If you sell a physical product, you should probably use a CPS model. If you provide a digital product or a service, then CPL *may* be appropriate.

CPS - cost per sale

Most standard affiliate programs use the CPS model. You only pay commission for a valid, shipped sale. This is a safe and simple way to encourage sales for your business.

Commission is paid:

- When an order has been shipped and the return window has expired

You can decline commissions:

- That are not shipped
- That are returned
- That don't follow the rules of your program
- That are later discovered to be fraudulent

Your validation process should take the customers' statutory rights into account. You should only approve commissions when you know the product can no longer be returned.

CPL - cost per lead

A lead is any action that can drive a commission. The commission is usually paid *even if* the lead doesn't turn into a valid order.

Commission can be awarded for:

- Completing an application for a service
- Completing a form to receive more information
- Placing an order (regardless of whether it ships)

You can only decline commissions that don't follow the rules of your program

6: Creating your program

You have decided to dip your toe in the warm waters of affiliate marketing. Welcome! Let's talk about what you need to consider and put in place to make it work for you.

Goals for this chapter

By the end of this chapter, you should be able to define the basic rules for your program, complete its technical requirements and populate your online profile.

Assumptions

This chapter will assume you have spent some time considering an affiliate program launch and that you have selected a partner network to run your program. You are now ready to start planning and building your new affiliate program.

Most SMEs launching a self-managed program use third-party e-commerce software such as Shopify or WooCommerce, so we will pay special attention to installation on these platforms.

This chapter will cover:

Top tip

Take your time. You can address all the points in this chapter in less than an hour, but the more time and thought you put into it, the better the results will be.

Plan to spend at least a day or two thinking about what you want from your program and what you need from your affiliates.

6.1 Commissions

The commission you pay is important because it motivates your affiliates to promote you. You have to make the program look like an opportunity without spending more than you can afford.

Goals for this section
This section addresses how much you pay affiliates for referring valid sales.

There are two main ways to calculate commissions. Other commission models are available, but they tend to fall outside the remit of self-managed programs.

Percentage

You can simply pay a percentage of the order value. This is the most common type of commission, and most self-managed programs will use this method to reward their publishers. To calculate a percentage commission, the order must have a defined order value, making it ideal for an outright purchase.

You do not have to pay commission on VAT or order costs (unless you want to), and most tracking plug-ins exclude VAT and delivery costs by default.

Fixed rate

Sometimes it is hard to assign an order value to a product, making it impossible to pay a percentage commission. Examples include mobile phone contracts and magazine subscriptions.

In such cases, you can pay a fixed commission. The fixed rate could be applied to each product in the order or to the whole transaction, depending on what you are selling.

Your priority

The affiliate earns a commission each time someone purchases after clicking their unique link. The commission rate is your main tool when it comes to rewarding affiliates. Your commission should:

- Look attractive to potential partners and inspire them to work hard on your behalf
- Achieve the goals of your program

New responsibility
Regularly review your commission rates to ensure they are still fit for purpose, which is to reward partners fairly for driving new customers to your website.

My goal is to make money, isn't it?

A lot of affiliate sales *don't* make any profit after the commission has been paid. That is OK *as long as* it is a conscious decision on your part. Is your priority to make more sales at any cost or to make a profit on every sale?

Think carefully about this point; a clear idea of what you want to achieve will make all future decisions much easier.

Choosing the right rate

Every affiliate program and vertical industry is different, so it is very hard to advise what commission you should pay.

The most important thing is that **you** should be happy with the rate you choose. You are the ambassador for your program, so you need to be able to present and justify the commission with confidence.

My competitor pays more than me - should I increase my commission rate?

You should be aware of what your competitors are paying, but don't feel compelled to increase your commission just because their rates are higher than yours. Only one merchant can deliver the highest rate in a particular sector, and other considerations matter just as much.

These include:

- Conversion rate
- Market position
- Supporting marketing
- Opportunities to increase sales when it really matters (seasonal events)
- Availability of promotional tools, such as voucher codes
- The proportion of your product range you pay commission on

If you have spent the time to build a complete offering, you will know exactly how to respond when an affiliate questions your rates.

That being said, if you can offer the highest rate *and* the most flexible partnerships, then you are in a firm position.

How do I know affiliates will like my rates?

As a rule of thumb, look at your average order value and what you expect your commission to be. How many of those commissions would make it worth an affiliate getting out of bed?

Your network may have some suggestions

While self-managed programs are self-service, it is in the network's interest to make sure you start on the right foot. Your integration manager may already have a commission rate in mind for your program.

You don't have to pay commission on VAT or delivery fees

It is standard practice to pay commission on the *subtotal* of the order before tax, VAT and postage fees. Most affiliate tracking plug-ins already take this into account.

The one commission group limitation

Commission groups control how much commission is paid for different sets of products.

Most self-managed programs only allow merchants to define one commission group. Even if your network doesn't have that restriction, it is still a good thing to aim for.

You can still decide whether to pay a fixed fee or a percentage of the order value, but whatever you choose will need to apply to all your products.

You *can* pay different affiliates different rates

You can choose to pay a specific affiliate or group of affiliates a different rate, as long as it applies to every product.

Some possible applications of this are:

- Increasing the commission for your top affiliates
- Giving an affiliate a temporary increase during a key promotion
- Decreasing the commission for an affiliate that offers an exclusive voucher code

What if I offer a free product?

You aren't obliged to pay if someone orders a free product unless it is a core aspect of your business.

In an ideal world, you should reward affiliates for everything your customers can order. That isn't always possible in the real world, but you do have to be fair.

A typical example is the mobile phone industry, where networks offer free SIM cards with €0 credit. Very few mobile networks reward affiliates when customers order these products.

If you have a product like this, you need to make it clear to your affiliates that it does not carry a commission and make sure it isn't in your product feed. Wherever possible, you should keep that free proposition away from the traffic your affiliates send to your site. It isn't fair to expect affiliates to promote the product if they won't be rewarded.

Top tip

Most affiliate platforms allow you to schedule commission changes at certain times. This is great if you want to support a seasonal event or reward a specific affiliate for increased coverage.

Front-end pricing should always track

Often, e-commerce sites will offer standard, publicly available offers and private, exclusive offers.

If a deal or offer is available to the general public and can be discovered on the front end of your website, then it should be eligible for commission.

Don't pay commission on gift cards

You should carefully consider whether to pay commission on the purchase of gift cards.

If you pay commission when a gift card is redeemed, you should **not** pay commission when the gift card is purchased.

A gift card with €10 of credit is still worth €10 after it has been purchased. If you offer commission (especially via cashback) when a customer purchases a gift card, and again when they spend the gift card in your checkout, it is possible to pay commission *twice* from a single purchase.

The industry calls this 'double dipping' because it is possible to earn commission twice on the same purchase. It used to be a popular loophole in the early days of cashback.

This also applies to other products that retain 100% of their face value, such as stamps or phone credit.

Your network should not penalise you for excluding these products from your affiliate program.

6.2 Building your proposition

Your proposition is a concise first impression of the service you provide and the rewards on offer. It describes and shapes the opportunity for your affiliates.

Goals for this section
This section will encourage you to spend extra time writing and maintaining your online profile.

Your default proposition

The **default proposition** is the first thing an affiliate sees when deciding whether to join your program. You may be prepared to be flexible, but the published terms form a lasting first impression. Therefore, it is important to get them right.

New responsibility
Communicate any changes to your proposition concisely and promptly to your affiliates.

Unrealised potential

Your default proposition provides a starting point for your relationship with your affiliates, but the best results will only be uncovered when you start working closely together.

If you (the advertiser) and your publishers both rely on your default propositions, there is probably unlocked potential in the relationship. Get in touch and start a conversation about what they need and value.

What does a good proposition look like?

Here is an example of a good proposition:

- We will pay **X%** of the sale value when you refer a customer

This simple statement is easy to understand and digest.

Compare it with the following terms based on an established affiliate program.

We will pay:

- **X%** on some products
- **Y%** on other products
- Nothing for *this* category
- Nothing for customers who have purchased from us before
- Nothing for customers who pay using credit

Self-managed programs should strive to be approachable and accessible. Too many conditions or restrictions can confuse publishers and make the program hard to manage.

Supporting material

While your online profile **explicitly** communicates your proposition, the other resources you provide **implicitly** support it.

Make sure your banners, creatives and product feeds reinforce the key selling points of your affiliate program, and don't contradict it with ambiguous messages or pricing.

Top tip

Practise explaining your proposition to anyone you can. Friends, colleagues, the dog... Does it make sense to someone who doesn't know about affiliate marketing?

6.3 Your online profile

Every network provides an online directory to help affiliates discover and engage with advertisers. This is the first thing a potential affiliate sees, so it is essential to make a good impression.

Goals for this section
This section will encourage you to spend extra time writing and maintaining your online profile.

How do I update my online profile?

All affiliate networks provide an editing tool for you to create your profile description. This may be a simple text editor, a WYSIWIG editor or a limited html editor.

Remember: you can change your profile

Your online advertiser profile is a living document that can grow and change with your program. You should check your profile regularly and update it based on feedback.

If you receive a lot of enquiries about a detail that you feel your profile already explains, it might be time to review your profile to see if it requires further explanation.

New responsibility
Keep your online profile up to date with the latest information about your proposition and the commission you pay.

What should be in the profile?

Your profile does not have to be a long document. A few paragraphs are usually more than enough.

It should cover the following points:

- A brief introduction to your business
- A summary of the products you sell
- A summary of the commissions you pay
- A summary of the most important limitations
- A description of the tools and resources you make available for your publishers
- A short description of what you value most in a partner
- Important information specific to your business or industry

Check the formatting

For security reasons, you can only use a limited set of formatting options or HTML tags. Once you click 'save', the online editor will double-check your content and delete anything that may be risky. In the process, the appearance of the text may change. Make sure you check the final product to make sure it matches what you had in mind.

Make sure every description makes sense on its own

Your network may ask for several descriptions and summaries of your program. These will be used on different pages in the network platform, often without any other context, so make sure each piece of content makes sense on its own.

Clearly describe what you sell

This may sound obvious, but you would be amazed at how many merchants don't describe the product or service they offer.

Compare these examples:

> “Ourbrand.co.uk is a leading telecommunication distributor. We aim to deliver the best customer service and have a 5* ReviewPilot rating.

> “Ourbrand.co.uk sells a wide selection of competitively priced SIM-free mobile phones. Prices start at €20 and go all the way up to €1,200 for the latest iPhones.

The first is an emotive description of the company's values, while the second accurately describes what it sells.

Both help the affiliate decide to promote the company’s program in different ways, so why not combine the two statements as follows?

> “Ourbrand.co.uk is a leading telecommunication specialist. We sell a wide selection of competitively priced SIM-free mobile phones, from €15 handsets to €1,200 iPhones. We aim to deliver the best customer service and have a 5* ReviewPilot rating.

Top tip

Online text and html editors sometimes experience issues that could delete your content.
You may find it useful to make a backup or copy the content to your clipboard before you click ‘save’.

Safety and security

Duplicate content

The best affiliates create their own unique content, but some affiliates re-use the content in your profile on their websites. Google and other search engines reward unique content, and their systems may penalise content they have seen before. Don't copy or re-use content from your website - write it specifically for your profile.

View your profile as an affiliate

The online interface doesn't always make it clear how your information will be presented to affiliates. It's a good idea to sign up for a publisher account, so you can see how it looks to your potential affiliates. Some networks provide a 'test' affiliate account specifically for this purpose.

Your online profile may be publicly available

Most networks make advertiser profiles available without logging in to their platform.

This is very useful because you can direct potential visitors to this page to learn more about your program and sign up.

However, some information should be reserved for enrolled affiliates. For example, some advertisers publish a link to their direct data feed, which is best restricted to members of your affiliate program.

Don't forget to check the publicly available page to make sure the information is suitable and performs its main role, which is to convince potential partners to apply to your program.

6.4 Program policies

One of the first challenges when creating a new program is deciding precisely what to allow your affiliates to do. You have to set enough rules to protect your business but leave affiliates enough room to be creative and proactive.

Goals for this section
After completing this section, you should be able to set the main rules and conditions that govern how affiliates can promote your brand.

Your terms and conditions help affiliates understand the rules they must follow to receive commissions. Partners have to accept these rules when they join your program.

If one of your affiliates infringes the rules, a well-written set of terms and conditions will help you to justify suspending or removing them from the program.

It is normal to set restrictions for:

- Type of affiliate allowed to promote your program
- Paid media
- Offline activity
- Voucher codes
- Permission to use your brand name

Please note

Where possible this book lists each task and milestone in the order you need to complete them. However, you may benefit from also reading the "**Types of affiliates**" chapter before you finalise your affiliate specific policies.

Where do I update my terms?

Most networks provide two places to set your terms:

- A dedicated control panel in your network interface
- A free text area for extra rules and conditions

You will probably have to use both tools to communicate everything effectively.

In addition, you can add the most important rules to the welcome email that is sent to affiliates when they join your program.

Top tip

Repetition is good. Repeating important rules makes them more likely to be read and understood. You can put the most critical points in your welcome email.

Sample policies

These policies should serve as a starting point for the myriad of permissions and privileges you can grant to affiliates. Each category has been given a recommendation based on how open or conservative you want to be in your approach to each type of promotion.

Each promotion type is given three recommendations to reflect how much control you have over each method - 'conservative', balanced and 'open'.

For most programs a 'balanced' approach is appropriate, but if you wish to be cautious the 'conservative' option may be more suitable. Conversely, 'open' opens the door even wider, permitting more partners and hopefully making more sales, at the cost of some control.

New responsibility

Make sure the affiliates that are enrolled to your program adhere to the rules and policies described in your online profile.

Vouchers

Conservative	Balanced	Open
✗	✓	✓

Considerations

- Can voucher affiliates promote your brand on Google Ads and other display networks?
- Can affiliates republish every promo or voucher code which your business creates?
- Should affiliates only publish codes which are approved for the affiliate channel?

Sub-networks

Conservative	Balanced	Open
✗	–	✓

Considerations

- Can affiliates enable sub-affiliates to promote your brand using their affiliate link?
- Should sub-networks make available a list of all sub-affiliates?
- Should all sub-affiliates be approved by the advertiser (whitelist)
- Are anonymous sub-affiliates permitted (blind sub-networks)?

Open Cashback

Conservative Balanced Open

Considerations

- Can affiliates return the commission you pay to their members as cashback or other rewards?
- Are any products or commissions unsafe for cashback?

Closed Cashback/loyalty

Conservative Balanced Open

Considerations

- Can affiliates return the commission you pay to their members as loyalty points or other redeemable rewards?

Display/native advertising

Conservative | Balanced | Open

Considerations

- Can affiliates send PPC traffic from display ads directly to your website?
- Can affiliates promote your brand on Google Display Network and other display networks?
- Can affiliates promote you on native content networks?
- Should display affiliates use approved creatives?

PPC

Conservative | Balanced | Open

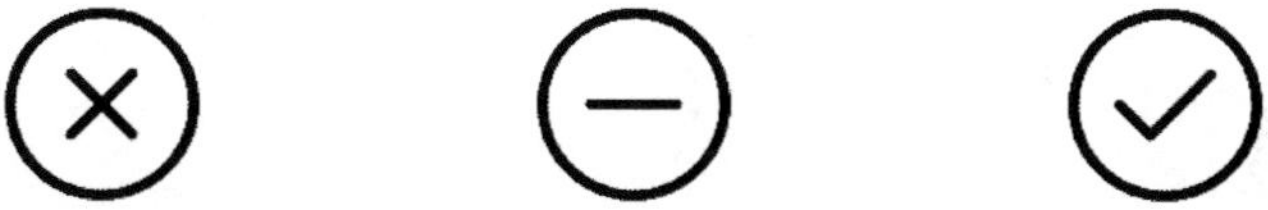

Considerations

- Can affiliates promote your brand via PPC?
- Can affiliates send PPC traffic directly to your website?
- Can affiliates bid for PPC ads using your brand name as a keyword?
- Can affiliates use your brand name in ad copy?
- Can affiliates use your domain name as the ad's 'display URL'?
- Can affiliates bid on misspellings of your brand name?
- Can affiliates target searches for your brand name plus other words or phrases?

Email

Conservative	Balanced	Open
⊗	⊖	✓

Considerations

- Can affiliates promote your brand to their email subscribers?
- Do affiliates need to adhere to the Controlling the Assault of Non-Solicited Pornography and Marketing Act (CANSPAM) or other regulations?
- Does email content need to be approved before it is sent?

Comparison shopping services (CSS)

Conservative	Balanced	Open
⊖	✓	✓

Considerations

- Can affiliates promote your brand in Google Shopping and similar services?

6.5 Banners and creatives

Pre-made banners and creative assets help affiliates promote you quickly and easily.

Goals for this section
This section should give you an understanding of why banners are important for your program and what resources you will need to provide to your publishers.

Does anyone use banners anymore?

For years, banner images were a very important part of affiliate marketing. Modern affiliate marketing no longer relies on banners as heavily as marketers did in the past, but they are still a very important asset for many publishers.

New responsibility
Make sure the image resources you provide are always up to date.

The most important creative: your logo

Your logo is one image that most affiliates can use. Make sure its design is crisp and clear, and make it available in various sizes. Try to offer versions that work on both dark and light backgrounds.

You don't want affiliates to make their own version of your logo, as they may do a poor job and potentially harm your brand perception.

An important branding exercise

Brand names can help establish credibility, so some advertisers like to use banners with prominent logos and brand messages to back up their own content. You can encourage this by issuing banners *without* calls to action like "click here" or "buy now".

Banner sizes

You can upload images of any size to your network, but most publishers use standard Internet Advertising Bureau (IAB) sizes.

The following sizes accounted for 90% of display advertising in 2021. Even if you don't permit affiliates to promote your business using display advertising, you should offer these sizes to stay compatible with on-site placements.

Banners are measured in pixels, and are presented as width × height:

- 300×250 (Medium Rectangle)
- 728×90 (Leaderboard)
- 160×600 (Wide Skyscraper)
- 300×600 (Half Page)
- 320×50 (Mobile Leaderboard)

In addition, you should offer these sizes to embed in editorial content:

- 468×60 (Banner)
- 970×90 (Large Leaderboard)
- 250×250 (Square)

You can find a full list of IAB sizes here:

https://www.iab.com/wp-content/uploads/2019/04/IABNewAdPortfolio_LW_FixedSizeSpec.pdf

High-resolution images

Affiliates may ask for a **high-resolution** or **vector** version of your logo. Some advertisers may be nervous about making such a powerful artistic asset freely available because it could be used for various purposes.

If you have any concerns, remember that you don't have to make high-resolution assets available to everyone - you can simply send them on a case-by-case basis.

Safety and security

Don't include web addresses in banners

If possible, don't include URLs in your creative elements. Affiliates like to be reassured that they will be rewarded for promoting your brand. If your banners display a full web address, such as 'www.example.com', there is a chance visitors could type it in manually without clicking the affiliate tracking link.

Replace banners, don't delete them

Your banners are hosted on the network's media server, which has the advantage of letting you see how many times the banner is served (the number of impressions).

Deleting an old banner image could cause your affiliates' pages to appear broken. If you replace or overwrite the banner, the old message is replaced with something more current.

If you do need to delete old banners, you should use the **impressions report** in your network reporting to be sure they are no longer in use.

Top tip

Banners often become out of date. Consider maintaining one group of banners called 'current promotion'. You can then simply update the images to reflect your current promotion, and the change will automatically be reflected on your publishers' websites.

6.6 Installing affiliate tracking

The tracking script is what makes your affiliate program possible. In keeping with the self-service ethos of self-managed programs, it is usually the advertiser's responsibility to install and test the tracking.

Goals for this section
This section should equip you to identify the best way to install the tracking script and how to test your tracking to ensure publishers can start sending traffic to your site.

Every network has a different integration process, but the common steps can be boiled down to the following:

- Install tracking on your website
- Click an affiliate link
- Make a test purchase
- Confirm the sale has been tracked by logging into your network
- Cancel the sale and make sure you don't get charged for the order
- Confirm the evidence with your integration manager

Top tip
A lot of networks make their installation instructions publicly available so you can review them before you select a network.

You will receive an integration manager

Each network uses a slightly different process to verify your tracking, but they will all provide a point of contact to guide you through the process.

It will be their responsibility to make sure you understand the rules of your network, verify that your tracking installation is complete and make the final decision to launch your program.

The confirmation page

To track a commission, you need to provide the affiliate tracking script with several key pieces of information:

- The value of the order
- A unique order ID
- Confirmation that the order has been completed and cannot be changed

The page that contains all this information is usually the **order confirmation** or **thankyou page** that customers receive after completing an order.

Some e-commerce platforms feature several confirmation pages - for example, for different payment methods. In such cases, you should make sure the tracking is included and functions separately for each version of the confirmation page.

New responsibility

Find out which page(s) of your checkout process cause a sale to track. It will be very useful in identifying possible tracking issues.

Tracking plug-ins

It may not be necessary to enlist a programmer to install the tracking on your website. Many popular e-commerce platforms support plug-ins that do all the hard work for you.

Most networks provide plug-ins for platforms like Shopify, which means you can install tracking on your site in seconds. A range of third-party plug-ins are also available, offering tracking for a variety of platforms.

Official plug-ins are best

If an official plug-in is available, try that first. It has been proven to work with your network and comes free of charge.

Third-party solutions come from an unverified source and may not be updated as promptly as official ones, but they can work well if you choose carefully. A confident e-commerce professional should be happy using either, but it is advisable to stick to the official plug-ins if you are less sure.

Plug-ins aren't always suitable

Plug-ins tend to cater for the most common use cases. If your requirements aren't quite standard, you may be out of luck.

For example, some plug-ins don't allow you to pay commission on the order subtotal, *including* VAT. If you encounter this, don't worry; the networks also provide step-by-step instructions to manually install and customise the tracking.

Google Tag Manager (GTM)

GTM is a powerful **container tag** that allows you to add tags to any page of your website without changing the code. It is still better to install the tracking directly on your website, but if that isn't possible, GTM is a good alternative.

GTM is very popular and may already be installed on your website. Almost every network provides detailed instructions about how to install their tracking tags via GTM.

Supported platforms

Key

Plug-in available

Instructions for installation in GTM

Detailed Instructions available

	AWIN	grow by Tradedoubler	WEBGAINS
Prestashop	Plug-in available	Plug-in available; Detailed Instructions available	Detailed Instructions available
Shopify	Plug-in available; Detailed Instructions available	Plug-in available; Detailed Instructions available	Plug-in available; Detailed Instructions available
WooCommerce	Plug-in available; Detailed Instructions available	Plug-in available; Detailed Instructions available	Plug-in available; Detailed Instructions available
Magento 2.0,2.4	Plug-in available	Plug-in available; Detailed Instructions available	Detailed Instructions available
Lightspeed	Plug-in available; Detailed Instructions available	Plug-in available; Detailed Instructions available	Detailed Instructions available
BigCommerce	Plug-in available; Detailed Instructions available	Plug-in available; Detailed Instructions available	
ShopWare	Plug-in available	Plug-in available; Detailed Instructions available	Plug-in available
Squarespace	Detailed Instructions available		
Wix	Instructions for installation in GTM		
Xonic Solutions	Plug-in available		
Google Tag Manager	Detailed Instructions available	Detailed Instructions available	Detailed Instructions available

6.7 Testing your tracking

Once the tracking is installed you have to verify that it is working correctly.

The testing process for most self-managed programs is very straightforward:

- Install some monitoring software in your web browser
- Click an affiliate link
- Make a purchase
- Confirm the sale has been tracked by logging into the network
- Send the evidence to the network

New responsibility
Ensure that the affiliate tracking stays installed on your website and is not accidentally displaced or removed.

Is it really that easy?

Yes! The self-managed integration and testing process is designed to work for businesses with limited access to developers or programmers.

The self-service approach is quick and safe as long as:

- You pay commission on everything you sell
- All sales from all sources are eligible for commission
- You only sell products on your website and not via a dedicated phone app

If any of the above is not the case, speak to your integration manager to ensure that all your sales are integrated.

Some networks have even simplified the process further, with tracking tests carried out automatically by the tracking plug-in.

Attribution and deduplication

Established e-commerce websites often work with several marketing channels. Some advertisers even work with more than one affiliate network. This means they could pay more than one source for the same order.

- **Attribution** technology decides which channel(s) directed a customer to your site
- **Deduplication** is the process of cancelling commissions and sales from other channels

Together, attribution and deduplication help protect merchants from paying several different channels for the same customer or order.

Self-managed programs are not aimed at merchants with such advanced requirements.

Instead, it is assumed that:

- You pay the same commission rate for everything
- Everything will track
- Different groups of customers don't get different prices
- You don't work with other affiliate networks

Top tip

It is best to conduct test transactions on your 'live' website, so you know you are testing the same experience your users will experience.
However, don't forget to cancel and refund your test transactions, to avoid being charged.

Don't be tempted to cheat

When you are performing the tracking test, you might spot something you had forgotten or notice that, while most of the tracking worked, there is one little detail that still needs another tweak.

It is tempting to massage the evidence slightly to avoid having to repeat the test. After all, you're going to fix it anyway, right?

It's not worth it. The process is already very streamlined, so make your changes and do the test again as many times as you need to until you are completely happy. It won't take long.

Make sure you check the order value and VAT

You can pay commission on the order amount before or after VAT - it's up to you. Just make sure your choice is reflected in the tracking and communicated to the customer in the program information.

When the network checks your tracking evidence, it does not know how much commission you intended to pay. It's up to you to ensure the correct amount is tracked.

Keep track of upgrades

If the plug-in developer updates the plug-in, you should always check that it still works on your website. E-commerce platforms often use several plug-ins that may conflict with each other, so you should check everything still works after any significant update.

6.8 Product feeds

If you want affiliates to advertise your products and not just your brand, it is a good idea to give them a list of the products you sell. All networks make this easy using product feeds.

Goals for this section
After completing this section, you should understand why product feeds are valuable to affiliates and how to generate a product feed from your own website.

Steps to create a product feed

1. Generate a feed in your e-commerce software
2. Register the feed in your network
3. Map the fields in your feed to the fields in the network
4. Map your product categories to the network category tree
5. Decide how often to update your feed

Generating the feed

There are several ways to create a product feed.

Built-in features

Some e-commerce platforms can generate out-of-the-box product feeds.

Existing data

If you already provide product data to Google or another service, you may be able to use the same data for your affiliate product feed.

Plug-ins

If you are using an open-source or hosted e-commerce platform, such as Shopify or WooCommerce, there is almost certainly a plug-in available that will take care of everything for you.

There are a few places to find appropriate plug-ins:

- Plug-ins recommended by your affiliate network that work well with their system
- The marketplace or plug-in library maintained by your e-commerce provider
- Third-party repositories, such as CodeCanyon.net

Third Party providers

Third party providers are a good alternative to expensive in-house development. They use a range of techniques including scraping and web-APIs to retrieve products from your website.

Some 'entry-level' ecommerce providers such as Squarespace and Wix, have limited plug-in support and may require third parties to generate advanced product feeds.

Advanced third parties retrieve data from almost any source, and turn it into rich, detailed product data for almost any provider. A good third-party provider can function as an external development team that maintains and takes responsibility for all your product data requirements.

Alternatives

If the options above are not applicable, then there are a few others:

- Install third-party software on your server
- Program it in-house

Generating feeds

A handy list of feed support for popular self-managed networks.

Key

- Supported by tracking plug-in
- Additional plug-in required
- External service required

	AWIN	grow by Tradedoubler	WEBGAINS
Prestashop	Additional plug-in required	Supported by tracking plug-in	Additional plug-in required
Shopify	Additional plug-in required	Supported by tracking plug-in	Additional plug-in required
WooCommerce	Additional plug-in required	Additional plug-in required	Additional plug-in required
Magento 2.0, 2.4	Additional plug-in required	Additional plug-in required	Additional plug-in required
Lightspeed	Additional plug-in required	Additional plug-in required	Additional plug-in required
BigCommerce	Additional plug-in required	Additional plug-in required	Additional plug-in required
ShopWare	Additional plug-in required	Additional plug-in required	Additional plug-in required
Squarespace	External service required	External service required	External service required
Wix	External service required	External service required	External service required

Required and optional fields

Every product listing must include basic information, such as the product name, a unique ID and an image. The list of mandatory fields is surprisingly short, but there is a long list of optional fields to enrich your product listings.

The *minimum* requirements for a product feed are usually:

- Product name
- Product description
- Unique product code
- 'Deep-link' URL for the product
- URL for the product image
- Price

A good product feed will include much more information, including the product colour, product specs and delivery information.

Review your network's feed documentation and try to include as many optional fields as possible.

Registering the feed in your network

Every network has a bespoke feed system for uploading or registering the feed. There is no standardisation, so the best advice is to read your network's documentation. Don't worry; it isn't a complicated process.

Feeds can be provided to the network in several ways:

1. Retrieved from a URL on your website
2. Uploaded manually to the network
3. Retrieved from a ftp location
4. Automatically uploaded by the network tracking plug-in(some networks only)
5. Submitted via an API connection

The most common method is to retrieve the feed from an online location.

Mapping

There are two types of mapping: **column mapping** and **category mapping**.

- **Column mapping** decides what data is included in the feed
- **Category mapping** decides which category each product appears in

Every merchant, including your competitors, assigns their products to a shared category tree. This helps affiliates sort through the available products quickly and efficiently.

Category mapping allows an affiliate to request a feed for, say, 'printer consumables' and receive matching products from all the advertisers they promote.

Use detailed categories

A lot of retailers map every product they sell to a single category - for example, *Office Supplies* or *Home and Garden*. Sometimes this is due to the lack of detail in the product data supplied to them, but sometimes they are just cutting corners.

If you do have detailed category information for what you sell, take the time to match it to the most appropriate categories in your network.

Categories are usually based on a hierarchy. If a product is mapped to *Computers and Software > Peripherals > Printer Consumables*, an affiliate can choose products from the top-level (Computers and Software) or narrow the search to only return 'Printer Consumables'.

Out of stock items and stock levels

A standard product feed should only include items that are in stock and available to purchase. If your e-commerce software supports it, you may also wish to exclude products with very low stock levels.

Some product feeds include the amount of stock available. This is strictly optional, and you are not obliged to share this information if you don't want to.

Scheduled update times

Your affiliate network can retrieve your product data several times a day. You can change the times from the network interface, so think about when you change your prices.

For example, if you usually add new products and review prices around 11 am, an update at midday would pick up and publish your changes quickly and efficiently.

Top tip

If a top-performing affiliate relies on your feed, why not ask them when they update their site and set your update schedule to accommodate them?

Advanced schema

Product feeds can easily cope with most everyday retail products. However, some products, like mobile phones, have extra attributes that don't necessarily fit into a standard product feed. Categories like texts, minutes and data need columns that don't apply to typical retail products.

Different networks have different ways of accommodating this special information. If you don't sell standard retail products, you should discuss your options with your integration manager.

New responsibility

Ensure that every product in your product feed is eligible for commission and that changes to stock or prices are promptly reflected in your feed.

Product images - copyright issues

One of the key requirements of a product feed is an image of each product:

- You provide the URL of the image to the network
- Your network provides it to the affiliate
- The affiliate publishes it on their website

The image is usually the same image you feature on your website. This raises a question about permission and copyright. You might have permission to use the photos on your website, but do you have permission to distribute them to your publishers?

The issue of who owns the copyright on product images has not been addressed by the e-commerce industry in general, particularly affiliates. This rarely causes a problem, but it does happen. There have been instances where lawyers have contacted merchants and affiliates to claim damages or demand the removal of images.

You don't need to make sweeping changes based on a minimal risk, but have a quick think about these questions:

- Are any of your suppliers or manufacturers known to be highly protective of their images?
- Did any product images on your website come with any usage conditions?
- When you found the images for your website, did you download them from the Internet without really thinking about where they came from? Be honest.

If the answer to any of these questions is 'yes', then it may be prudent to seek further advice. In certain circumstances, it is worth considering changing the images you provide to affiliates.

Duplicate content

Product feeds usually use the content from your website, including product names and descriptions. A lot of affiliates may republish this content verbatim. This can be a problem if Google labels it as 'duplicate content', which is generally accepted to have a negative impact on SEO.

If possible, try to give affiliates an alternative or truncated version.

Avoid manual processes if you can

It is tempting to say, "I'll just update this spreadsheet and upload it when a price changes". Manual, ad hoc processes like this invariably fall by the wayside.

If you can avoid generating your product feed manually, you should. Plug-ins or third-party solutions to generate product feeds are inexpensive and could even give your business new capabilities and options in the future.

6.9 Google Analytics

It can be useful to see your affiliate traffic alongside your other marketing activity. Google Analytics (GA) makes this quick and easy.

Goals for this section
This section should provide a starting point for you to account for affiliate traffic in your Google Analytics installation.

GA4

We will concentrate on GA's latest version - GA4. Version 4 was released in late 2020, and at the time of writing, it is the preferred/default version when you log into GA. You can still use older versions for a limited time, but these will be removed in 2023.

As GA is the most popular analytics platform in the world, almost every e-commerce platform supports it with built-in features or plug-ins. There is an excellent chance you are already using GA, but it is easy to install and start using if you are not.

UTM Parameters

Google will always try to identify where traffic came from, but advertisers can make this easier and more reliable by adding some basic information to inbound links.

These extra pieces of information are called 'UTM parameters'.

UTM parameters have several benefits:

- They help distinguish sales from the affiliate channel
- They can tell you exactly which publisher or website referred a customer
- They make advanced techniques such as parameters A/B testing possible.

Wildcards

While it is good start to simply tell GA that traffic came from the affiliate channel, you can also provide detailed information about specific affiliates using wildcards. A wildcard is a symbol or phrase that can be replaced with dynamic information.

Most networks provide wildcards for common values such as the affiliate ID, affiliate name and affiliate promotion type. When the affiliate network sees a wildcard it will replace it with the appropriate value.

For example, '**%Affiliate_Name%**' might be replaced with '**TopDiscounts.com**', or '**%Affiliate_ID%**' might be replaced with '**56789**'.

Tracking affiliate traffic and sales in GA4

Every affiliate network can automatically attach custom UTM information to every affiliate click. This feature is very useful because if you asked affiliates to add the information manually, very few would do so.

Note that GA4 does not support as many UTM parameters as GA's previous versions, so we'll use three straightforward and common tags - source, medium and campaign.

Top tip

Keep things simple. Most networks provide a range of wildcards for information like the affiliate's name, promotion type, *etc.* Too much detail can make it very hard to perform meaningful analysis, so think about what you really need.

How do I implement UTM parameters?

Your network integration manager should be able to add these UTM parameters to your account quickly and easily, so discuss the options with them when you are setting up your program.

The simplest option

These UTM values will make sure GA knows a) the traffic came from an affiliate and b) which affiliate it was:

- **utm_source**: The referring channel - 'affiliate'
- **utm_medium**: The network name - 'Awin', 'Tradedoubler', 'Webgains'
- **utm_campaign**: A wildcard or dynamic value that supplies the unique ID for the affiliate that sent the traffic

Richer data

This option uses more dynamic information to show the type of activity the affiliate is carrying out. Please note that it is the publisher that informs the network of their promotion type, and this information may not always be accurate.

- **utm_source**: The referring channel - 'affiliate'
- **utm_medium**: A wildcard or dynamic value that returns the type of promotion the affiliate has told the network they carry out.
- **utm_campaign**: A wildcard or dynamic value that supplies the unique ID for the affiliate that sent the traffic

Anyone can add UTM tags to links

Remember, any website can add UTM tags to links, and they may not use the same format and conventions that you do. You can't change these UTM tags, so the information may appear in a different format.

The online review platform Trustpilot is a good example. When users click to view a business from a Trustpilot review, Trustpilot adds UTM information that tells GA business where the traffic was sent from.

Avoid UTM tags on internal links

It may seem like a good idea to add UTM parameters to links on your own website - for example, to record when someone clicked a homepage banner or clicked a specific link.

While self-managed programs rarely use attribution to decide whether to pay an affiliate commission, it is likely you may use Google Analytics for reporting and information purposes.

You should **never** use UTM tags on internal links.

UTM tags on internal links could cause Google to forget that a user came from an affiliate, leading you to undervalue the affiliate channel,

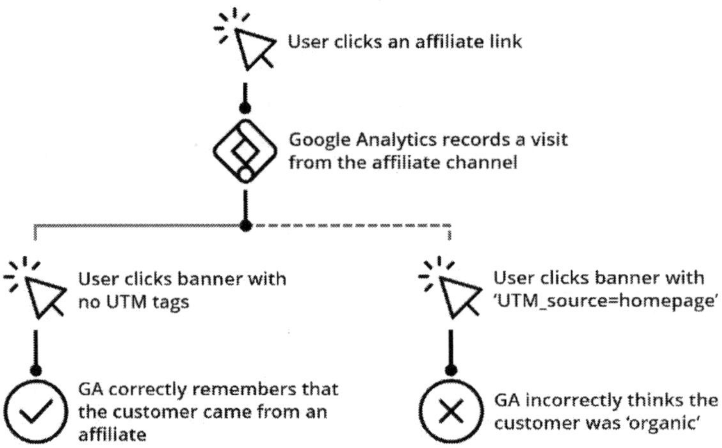

6.10 Optimising your website

Affiliates rely on your e-commerce website to convert traffic into sales. It is important to ensure it is prepared to convert these visitors into paying customers.

Goals for this section
This section should help you make sure your site is in the best position to convert affiliate-generated traffic into paying customers.

Address common leakage points

Leakage occurs when a publisher loses commission due to an error or untracked action on your website.

No e-commerce website is perfect, and even the most successful advertisers have niggles that affiliates don't like. The key is to keep these to a minimum and show that you are taking action when possible.

The following examples are the most common sources of leakage. Could any of them affect your affiliate program?

Prominent telephone numbers

Many e-commerce websites display a phone number for customers to ask questions and place orders. As you would expect, affiliates don't like this because they are only rewarded for *online* sales.

You can hide the phone number just for affiliate traffic with a straightforward piece of code. This solution, while not 100% effective, shows that you are making every effort to treat your affiliates fairly. You should ask whoever supports your e-commerce platform whether this is possible for your website.

At the very least, don't actively try to force visitors who were referred by affiliates to complete their purchase over the phone.

Off-site links

Affiliates send their traffic to you in the hope that it will convert into paying customers and generate commissions. You may have prominent links asking visitors to *leave* your website, such as:

- Links to partners or suppliers
- Links to other stores or websites owned by your company
- Affiliate links or links to other merchants

You don't have to remove every external link from your website, but you should try to separate them from pages which form the key shopping journey. It is generally OK to include content like this in your blog or news chapter.

Internal voucher codes

Many e-commerce websites promote modest voucher codes to reward actions like joining the newsletter or making a first purchase. Vouchers are a useful tool to help undecided customers convert.

These codes are likely to be used by a large percentage of your customers, so check whether affiliates will be rewarded when these publicly available voucher codes are used. You should always try to ensure your affiliates are fairly treated.

Alternate payment methods

Modern e-commerce sites often accept multiple payment methods, allowing customers to pay using credit/debit cards, gift cards, online wallets or 'buy now pay later' credit services.

Alternate payment services often modify your shopping cart or send customers to a different confirmation page once the order is complete, and it is relatively common for affiliate tracking to be omitted from these pages.

If you use a network-provided tracking plug-in, you should ask your integration manager if it has any limitations.

Tell people about your affiliate program

Your website can also help to recruit new affiliates to your affiliate program. Why not create a page listing the program's benefits and rewards, plus a link to your affiliate network?

You may have seen these links in the footer of popular e-commerce websites. It is not necessary to feature the link on every page of your site - it could be enough to only place it in the 'about us' chapter.

An 'our affiliate program' page appeals to different types of visitors:

- Web searches for 'yourbrand affiliate program'
- Affiliates that are actively checking if you have an affiliate program
- Affiliates who compulsively check every e-commerce site they visit for an 'affiliates' link (like the author of this book)
- Customers and visitors who are also influencers

New responsibility
Make sure affiliates are considered when you update or improve your website. Will the changes affect help or hinder their ability to earn commission?

7: The launch

Tracking... Check. Commissions... Check. Is it time? Are you ready to launch?

Goals for this chapter
This chapter should equip you to double-check your preparations and liaise with your affiliate network to launch your self-managed program.

This chapter will cover:

7.1 Launch checklist

First, give yourself a pat on the back. You are about to launch an entirely new marketing channel for your business! Of course, this is just the beginning. Once it is up and running, it is up to you to grab that opportunity and turn it into meaningful results.

Key

- Required
- Recommended
- Done by network
- Optional

	AWIN	grow by Tradedoubler	WEBGAINS
Introductory consultation		Required	Required
Review optional services	Recommended	Recommended	Recommended
Pay joining fee			
Supply monthly payment details	Required	Required	Required
Install tracking	Required	Required	Required
Install master container tag throughout site	Recommended	Recommended	Recommended
Test tracking	Required	Required	Required
Provide program logo	Required	Required	Required
Provide company details	Required	Required	Required

	AWIN	grow by Tradedoubler	WEBGAINS
Provide account contact details	✓	✓	✓
Set primary account contact	✓	✓	✓
Program description	✓	✓	✓
Short summary description	✓	✓	–
Define PPC policy	✓	✓	✓
Define voucher policy	✓	✓	✓
Define brand use policy	✓	✓	✓
Upload supporting documents	–		
Supply banners and creatives	✓	✓	✓
Upload email creative	–	–	–
Set commissions	✓	✓	✓
Enable affiliate auto-enrolment	–	–	–
Set auto-validation period	✓	👍	✓
Define cookie period	⊘	👍	👍
Customise welcome email	⊘	⊘	⊘

	AWIN	grow by Tradedoubler	WEBGAINS
Register product feed	⊘	⊘	⊘
Provide GA string to network	⊖	⊖	⊖
Register approved voucher codes	⊘	⊘	⊘
Register offers or promotions	⊘	⊘	⊘
Prepare site for pre-approved publishers		⊘	
Provide assets for pre-approved publishers		⊘	
Add key statistics to your profile and description		⊘	
Confirm mobile optimised status	👍		
Opt in or out of welcome email guides	⊘		
Conduct post-launch consultation		⊘	⊘

Who decides when the program is ready to launch?

The final green light is given by your network integration manager, but you should make sure you are prepared for the interest the launch generates. Therefore, the launch date should be mutually agreed between you and your integration manager.

Is there a good time to go live?

New programs launch every day of the week, so there isn't really a bad time to launch your program. Depending on the projected pattern of your sales, you may wish to aim for the start of the week to make time to reply to enquiries before the weekend.

Top tip
Don't aim to only complete the bare minimum requirements. Your online profile and the resources you provide will directly influence how many affiliates will want to promote you, so be as comprehensive as possible.

7.2 The first few days

When you launch a new program, it is vital to stay on top of the basics:

- Accept or reject affiliate applications daily
- Respond to any contact promptly
- Populate your profile completely
- Explain your commissions
- Provide accurate contact details

Log in every day during your launch period to answer any questions you are asked and research prospective affiliates before approving or rejecting applications. Even if you struggle with technical questions, showing you are engaged and responsive is the single best thing you can do to build trust with affiliates.

When your program launches, you will appear in your network's 'new merchants' list. This generates a lot of interest, and you will receive many applications in the first few days. Make the most of it by acting on those applications quickly.

It is up to you to decide which affiliate applications are genuine opportunities. Some of them will be speculative - a lot of affiliates just apply for every program they see - but others can be time-sensitive, perhaps to monetise a specific page or opportunity.

When will the sales start to roll in?

It can take a while for affiliates to incorporate your brand into their activities, especially if they rely on SEO. It isn't unusual to wait several weeks to see your first sales tracked on your affiliate network. Be patient, stay proactive, make sure you are meeting the requirements of your publishers, and you will be rewarded.

8: Recruiting affiliates

Congratulations! Your affiliate program is live to the world. Now the hard work starts - using the building blocks provided by your network to build a successful affiliate program.

Goals for this chapter

Your affiliate program needs publishers to succeed. This chapter describes how to process applications to your program and how to identify and recruit top-performing partners.

This chapter will cover

Assumptions

The next two chapters will assume that you have recently launched an affiliate program. Your priority now is to recruit affiliates, discover new opportunities and make sales for your business.

8.1 Affiliate applications

You must review and approve each affiliate that wants to promote you before they can earn commissions. First impressions are important, so it's a good idea to review your pending applications as quickly as possible.

Goals for this section
In conjunction with the chapter on affiliate types, this section should equip you to make safe decisions when considering inbound applications to promote your program.

Research affiliates before you approve them

Don't be tempted to just accept (or reject) every application without researching it first. Some of your applications will be from sites that won't benefit your brand, but there are some genuine opportunities that may not be apparent at first glance.

New responsibility
Review and process applications for your program regularly.

It is OK to say no

You don't have to accept every application you receive. Simply reject any application you don't think fits your requirements and concentrate on the applications you are more comfortable with. It doesn't help anyone if you leave the application pending.

How relevant does an affiliate need to be?

One of the main reasons to reject an affiliate is 'this site is not relevant to my product'.

Context can make up for lack of direct relevance. For example, if you sell drones and a mobile phone affiliate applies to your program, there could be a good reason. They may have some insight about their audience that you aren't aware of, or they could be writing an article about fun accessories that work with mobile phones. While their website may not appear relevant, some of their content may be.

Remember, you can always contact the affiliate to ask for more information about their application.

Choose a detailed rejection reason

The affiliate platform allows you to accept and reject affiliates quickly and easily.

When you reject an application, you will be asked to select a reason from a pre-defined list of reasons like 'we don't work with this type of affiliate' or 'not relevant to our product'.

You might be wrong

Affiliates don't always keep their network profiles up to date, or their business name may not reflect what they actually do. It is very easy to reject genuine opportunities inadvertently.

Keep your communication polite and professional when you reject affiliates in case you change your mind later.

Auto-enrolment

Most networks offer the facility to automatically accept all applications to your program. That means publishers can start promoting you immediately, and it can help you to build a large database of affiliates quickly.

However, most of the advice in this section - and indeed the entire book - is based around being *selective* to focus on the best opportunities and protecting your program and brand. This gives you the opportunity to research your partners and the peace of mind that you are in control of how you are represented online.

Most affiliate programs and program managers benefit from reviewing and understanding affiliates before they can start earning commission.

Affiliate profiles aren't always up to date

Every network provides a simple profile system to help affiliates introduce themselves and describe what they do. They can be very useful, but as mentioned above, they are often not 100% complete.

Publishers often run several websites - sometimes even hundreds of them. Don't assume the property listed in the network interface is the one they intend to promote you from. If in doubt, you can always reach out to the affiliate for more information.

A reasonable default acceptance policy

This reasonably conservative acceptance policy exposes you to the biggest opportunities and shields you from potential risks.

Accept:

- Content sites
- Social media channels with a verifiable presence
- Price comparison platforms
- Large, organised cashback sites
- Employee benefits services
- Reputable voucher sites with a unique selling point

Be more cautious of:

- Voucher sites with no traffic or unique selling point
- Social media affiliates that hide behind closed groups, where you can't see or review the activity
- Social media affiliates that rely on private messages
- Toolbars and browser extensions
- PPC/paid affiliates that require 'brand bidding' permission
- Anyone who doesn't clearly state what they do
- Small cashback sites that may not have the resources or expertise to offer cashback safely

Who can accept affiliates onto my program?

When an affiliate applies to your program, they agree to your terms and conditions and promise to follow all current and future rules. In return, you agree that the activity they have declared is acceptable and promise to treat them fairly.

Only you or your authorised agents should approve affiliates. Every affiliate should apply to your program personally and be approved by you. That is the only basis for a safe and fair affiliate program.

8.2 Outbound recruitment

When your program first launches, you will receive a lot of applications from potential affiliates. After a while, the quality of applications will start to decline. That is the time to actively research the market and let people know about your new program.

Goals for this section
This section will help you prepare for the next stage of affiliate recruitment - approaching potential partners to grow your program.

Official invitation emails

Every affiliate network offers an 'invite' feature to recruit new affiliates quickly. You can browse every affiliate on the network and choose which ones to contact. These systems need to work for thousands of merchants and affiliates, so they aren't very personalised.

This official network feature should be your first port of call, but be prepared to follow it up with a more tailored message. If you are particularly keen to recruit an affiliate, it may pay to contact them first and only send the invite when you know they will accept it.

New responsibility
Research and contact potential affiliates on a regular basis.

Don't just invite everyone

Don't be tempted to invite thousands of affiliates in the hope that some will be relevant. Affiliates frown upon this approach, and it is a sure-fire way to attract poor-quality partners.

Top tip

You could start outbound recruitment from day one, but it may pay to wait a short while. Use the first few days to iron out the glitches and fine-tune your program.

You can recruit affiliates into the affiliate industry as well as your program

Let's imagine you find an amazing website with lots of visitors that would be the perfect ambassador for your products. However, you aren't sure if they use affiliate marketing. They might make money using different methods, or perhaps they don't monetise their site at all.

Don't be put off. In fact, this is the time to get excited - you have just discovered a new untapped opportunity that could turn into a very lucrative partnership.

Respect their values

If the publisher uses sentiments like 'independent' or 'unbiased' to describe themselves, you don't want to contradict them or imply that they have to compromise their beliefs to work with you.

Use their language

The affiliate industry tends to use words like 'visitors' or 'consumers' to describe customers, but an influencer or blogger may prefer to think of them as 'readers', 'subscribers', or even 'friends'.

Give them a clear next step

If you are sending an unsolicited message, you can't tell your new prospect what to do, but you can make a suggestion. Offer to set up a call or send more information if they are interested, always including a tangible 'next step' to change the communication from an unsolicited message to a conversation.

Telephone is not always the best contact method

Calling affiliates is the most direct way to contact and speak to new prospects. Some affiliates respond well to phone calls, while others may find them annoying or intrusive.

A lot of affiliate profiles list 'telephone' as the preferred contact method, but this is the default contact option for all new accounts on some platforms. It may be correct, or it could just mean the user hasn't customised their profile yet.

Top tip
Some affiliate networks require affiliates to pass extended security checks or pay a small charge to join. This is good because it protects the industry, but it makes it hard to invite new affiliates. Your network may be able to waive these charges to make it easier for a new partner to join. Contact your network to see what is possible.

8.3 Another way to think of affiliates

There are many types of affiliate activity - cashback, voucher, search, *etc.* Here is a different way to think of your potential partners.

Affiliates that need you more than you need them

These partners tend to be attracted by your brand. Working with you lends them credibility. They may not deliver many sales yet, but they are hopeful.

These affiliates are usually more prepared to deviate from their standard offering and shouldn't demand too much in return.

Often, making sales isn't their main priority. Some of these publishers are more interested in associating with other brands because of how it looks than generating revenue. Be cautious of publishers that are also merchants selling their own products.

Some of these affiliates can be great partners, but they also take time to manage. There are thousands of these 'long tail' affiliates - the trick is picking the right ones to concentrate on.

Affiliates that you need more than they need you

These are more established affiliates with established sites and verifiable sales. You know they can make sales in volume, and you want a slice of that action. In this case, working with them enhances your credibility.

Partners like these find brand names useful, but they only covet hugely recognisable or popular brand names. You are more likely to have to accept their default product or pay for access. Getting more coverage is generally streamlined and might involve choosing from a rate card or a clearly defined list of partnership options.

These affiliates generally know what they are doing and don't take much time to manage at first. That changes when you start working closely with them, but since that should lead to lots of new sales, it's a nice problem to have.

Which one do I need?

Both, of course! However, connecting to established sites with existing traffic and demand is the best route to success in the first instance. Such partners are a proven quantity that you know can make sales. It can take a while to recruit them, so get started as soon as possible.

Worthwhile targets include:

- Established mainstream cashback sites
- Large employee benefits sites
- Price comparison platforms (if they exist in your industry)

The easiest way to recruit these affiliates is often an introduction from your network account manager. However, that isn't possible with most self-managed programs, so you will need to make the approach yourself. You should be able to find the affiliate's contact details in the network interface.

8.4 Protecting your brand

Brand names are the basis of a large percentage of activity in the affiliate industry- whether that means your business brand or the names of the products you sell.

Goals for this section
This section aims to encourage you to think about the power of your brand name and how it can be used to empower affiliates.

Your brand is valuable

Brand names are desirable. Affiliates value brand names because they provide something solid that they can build their activity around.

By focusing on your brand name, the affiliate benefits from the effort you have put into building your reputation. As your brand becomes more popular, it attracts more traffic, and you make more sales. With a recognisable brand name, affiliates can easily:

- Build a page on their website that competes with your official site on Google - if they have a popular website and yours is quite new, it could easily appear above your own in the search listings
- Build pages with the brand name in the URL and page titles
- Rank in search engines for 'brand' + voucher code terms
- Pay for PPC ads that target your brand name

Some of the above actions are in your interest; others may not be. The affiliate manager's job is to say yes to as many opportunities as possible without damaging your brand.

Brand-related decisions you make now can stick with you for a long time

Let's imagine you launch a program and 100 voucher websites apply to join it. You don't even provide voucher codes, but you might in the future, and it's positive activity, right?

Well, yes - getting any affiliate to do anything is a forward step. But now, 100 websites could be competing with your site when someone searches for your brand online.

Since you don't offer voucher codes, those 100 results could contribute to a negative or frustrating experience for the user.

If visitors perceive the results as 'low value' or 'not useful', that could put them off your brand completely.

You can reject affiliates if you don't like their coverage, but you can't be sure all the problematic content will get removed. It is safer to avoid the issue by not accepting them in the first place.

9: Types of affiliates

Affiliate programs attract publishers with different priorities and methods of achieving their goals. This chapter will discuss the different types of affiliates in detail.

Goals for this chapter

The affiliate landscape is incredibly diverse. Each sections in this chapter introduces the most common types of affiliates, their strengths and weaknesses and how to increase their contribution to your program.

This chapter will cover:

Classifications

Publishers

Please note

The recommendations in this chapter are based on an overall view of the industry. Individual affiliates may present a different proposition and opportunity.

9.1 Traffic types

Any affiliate can make a significant contribution to your program - you just need to decide which types of traffic you value.

Direct

Direct affiliates deal in traffic rather than content, and their preference is to send traffic straight to your website. These affiliates' audiences and traffic are often obtained using paid media and search engine marketing.

Unqualified

Affiliates don't have to know about the products they are promoting. As they are likely to be working with a large number of affiliate programs, they may choose which brands to promote based on the potential reward rather than the topic. Their SEO footprint is often based on brand names, so they are the least likely to make credible recommendations about your product or service.

Topic expert

Topical traffic comes from affiliates and websites that have a link or relationship to the product they are promoting. They may not have the authority or influence to make trusted recommendations, but they can refer high-quality, relevant traffic. They are more likely to appear in Internet searches for keywords related to your products, not just your brand name.

Authority

A publisher that is very closely related to your product or service can provide recommendations and endorsements that carry weight. Their experience and expertise in your industry help shape their content, making them trusted sources of information for consumers. Because they are judged on their recommendations and advice, they protect their reputation by selecting their partners carefully.

9.2 Strengths and weaknesses

Different affiliates have different strengths. As a rule, most default propositions do not have all three strengths.

Each affiliate type has been given a rating to show their weakest point, with suggestions on how to remedy it.

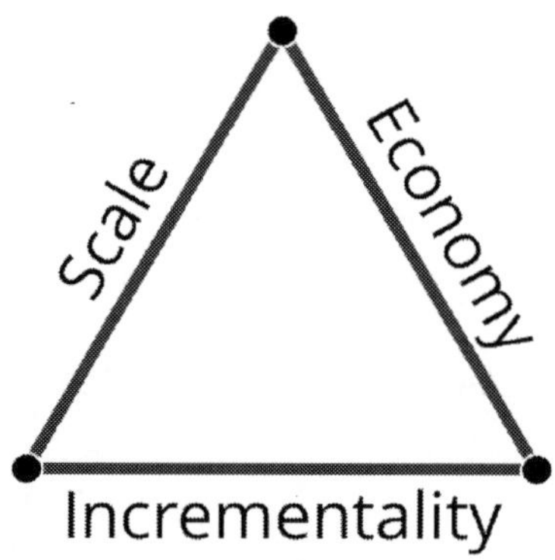

Scale

Some affiliates are capable of delivering large volumes of traffic immediately.

Economy

Some channels are more cost-effective than others.

New customers

Some promotion methods help you to reach new customers, while others may favour people who are more familiar with your brand and products, a distinction known as **incrementality.**

9.3 The Conversion Funnel

Almost all digital marketing channels use the funnel to describe the customer's purchasing journey.

There are multiple versions of the funnel, some with more stages than others. We're going to discuss a simple version with just four stages.

Professionals on every side of the affiliate industry – networks, agencies and publishers, all refer to the conversion funnel.

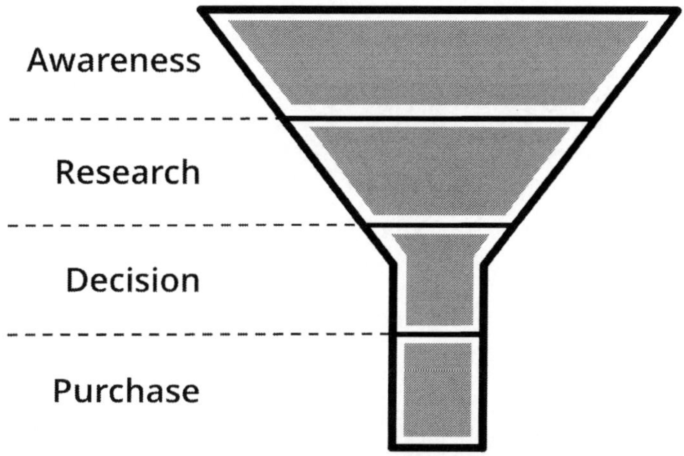

Every type of publisher in the following pages has been given a rank to show where in the conversion funnel they interact with potential customers.

Remember, these are arbitrary descriptions that are reflect the industry as a whole. Individual publishers may offer different (hopefully better) value.

Awareness

The consumer is exposed to a product or topic and finds it interesting.

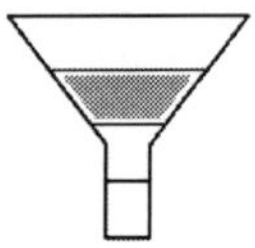

Research

The consumer's interest advances from general interest to more active involvement and research. Is this product right for them? Which one should they buy?

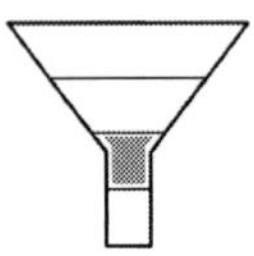

Decision

The consumer has decided to make a purchase, and they are actively thinking about which model to buy and who to purchase from.

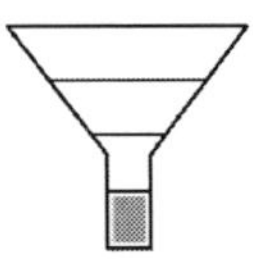

Purchase

All the decisions have been made - the focus is now on completing the purchase.

Some affiliate types are given more than one funnel position, to indicate that they can influence multiple stages of the purchasing journey.

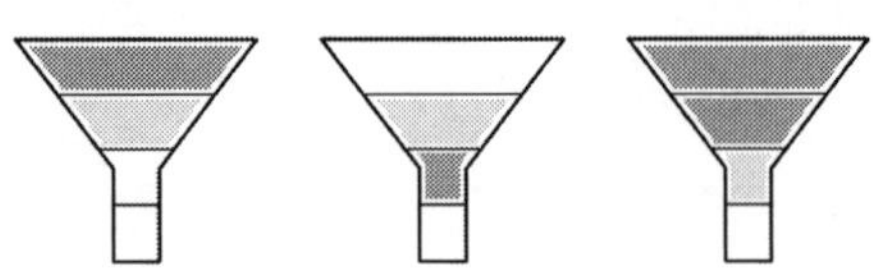

Why is the funnel relevant to affiliate marketing?

While there are exceptions, different types of affiliates are often perceived as occupying certain levels of the funnel. For example, bloggers and influencers are usually understood as 'upper funnel' partners, while cashback and voucher sites are usually deemed 'lower funnel'. An effective affiliate program combines affiliates from every level of the funnel.

It is easier to identify and target consumers as they reach the end of the purchasing journey, so the most successful affiliates often target the bottom of the funnel.

Customers frequently turn to mechanisms like cashback and vouchers *after* they have made the decision to purchase. An efficient lower funnel can help influence undecided consumers and make sure they purchase from you and not your competitors.

'Upper funnel' publishers are often sensitive about their commission being claimed by other affiliates. Tools such as assisted commissions can help reassure them that they will be fairly rewarded for their efforts.

While there are more potential customers at the top of the funnel, it is hard to target them accurately - it is usually easier to identify customers who are at the bottom of the funnel.

As they get closer to making a purchase, the funnel narrows and the potential audience decreases, but the likelihood that the consumer will make a purchase increases.

Consumers don't have to enter at the top of the funnel. If they already know they need a product or service - for example, travel insurance for their next holiday - they may go straight to 'research' or even 'decision'.

9.4 Cashback and incentive sites

Cashback and incentive sites are often the top-performing affiliates on a network. They pass the commission they receive from you back to the customer as cash, vouchers or goods.

What do they do?

Cashback and incentive sites pay their members a portion of the money they earn from affiliate commissions. Customers make their purchase from your online store and receive cash back, hence the name.

Unqualified traffic | Decision / purchase stage

How do cashback sites know which member to reward?

The cashback mechanism uses a small piece of information called the **click-ref**.

1. When a reward affiliate displays the link to one of its members, it is customised with a click-ref - a string or number that is unique to that member
2. The affiliate tracking cookie remembers the click-ref
3. When the customer makes a purchase, the stored click-ref is associated with that sale
4. When the affiliate is paid its commission, the same click-ref is included in the reporting, which the affiliate can use to identify the member who initially clicked the link

Click-refs are very simple but very useful. Without this essential mechanism, incentive sites would not be possible.

All networks support at least one click-ref. Some allow affiliates to add multiple click-refs to the same link.

How much do cashback sites give back?

The most popular cashback sites give back 100% of the commission they receive, while others may pass on 50% or 80% of the commission.

Both models have benefits and disadvantages. Full cashback is more attractive to the consumer, while partial cashback sites give the publisher more flexibility to offer coverage without asking for tenancy payments.

Services that offer 100% cashback usually only pass the *base* commission rate to their members. If the commission is increased due to performance tiers or bonuses, the affiliate can decide whether to keep the extra commission or share it with its members.

Working with cashback affiliates

What cashback affiliates value most

Like voucher and deal affiliates, cashback sites look for ways to stand out. Since they pass a lot of their commission to their members, they also value other ways to earn revenue.

Cashback sites are usually looking for:

- Exclusive discounts
- Increased commission (to pass on as cashback)
- Willingness to pay marketing fees or tenancies

The best thing cashback affiliates can offer

Extra coverage should help introduce you to new consumers who may not have heard of your brand before. Others may be aware of your brand but aren't yet actively considering a purchase, and cashback could be the extra push they need.

How do cashback publishers make money?

If they give all their commission back to their members, how do cashback sites make any money?

- They only pay the 'base' commission rate to their members
- Tenancy payments
- Brand partnerships
- Performance bonuses
- Membership fees
- Unclaimed cashback
- Interest payments on unclaimed cashback

Incentives affect customer decisions

Cashback or other types of reward motivate the customer. When the reward is a big part of the purchase decision, we refer to the customers as being **incentivised**.

Incentivised customers can behave differently from other consumers. They may not be as loyal or use the product in the way you intended them to. If the reward is too attractive, they might not actually want your product at all, or they may just be purchasing it to resell it.

New responsibility
Make sure your processes and payment schedules enable customers to receive their cashback as quickly and smoothly as possible.

Open vs closed groups

Reward sites can serve the general public or a closed group with special entry requirements. While both approaches use similar technology to reward customers, they can behave and function quite differently.

Public cashback sites

Anyone can join a public cashback website. As a rule, they work with as many advertisers as possible and return the commission paid to them as cashback, vouchers or virtual currency.

Strengths and weaknesses

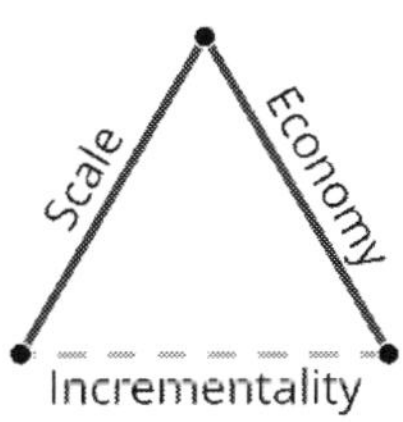

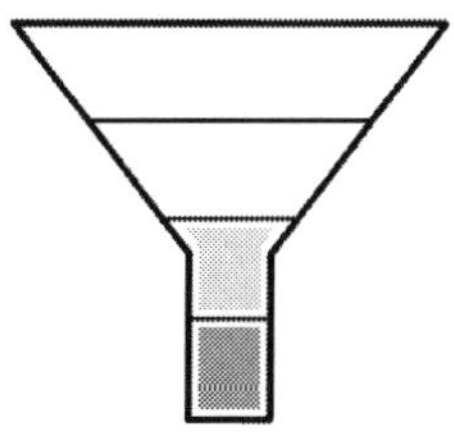

Cashback is attractive to customers who have already decided to purchase from you, so it is not always considered incremental by default.

You can influence this in several ways:

- Encourage placements on 'hub' or 'discovery' pages, as well as the page dedicated to your brand
- Use secure email coverage
- Consider incentives that favour or only work for new customers
- Encourage promotion of the cashback offer on other websites

The aim is to reach new people who may not have previously heard of your brand. This extra coverage may come at the cost of increased commission or a tenancy payment, so you need to make sure it is still within your means.

A reasonable acceptance policy for cashback affiliates

Cashback sites are an essential part of the shopping journey for many consumers. They help justify more expensive purchases, and when managed properly, they encourage the discovery of new products and brands. This policy exposes you to the most significant opportunities but also leaves you time to get the best value from them.

Default PPC rule

- Do not drive traffic using PPC

Vouchers to promote

- Only promote voucher codes that are authorised for the affiliate channel

Affiliates to accept

- At least one major public cashback site
- All in-house loyalty schemes - supermarkets, *etc.*

Affiliates to consider

- Other sites where the audience is relevant to your product

Affiliates to reject

- Small cashback services that may not be able to provide a consistent service to their members
- Cashback sites serving regions or countries that your business does not ship products to

'Closed group' cashback sites

Closed groups use cashback tracking to create a new proposition for their users. Membership may be open to anyone in a specific demographic or work on an invite-only basis for customers of a specific service or members of a specific organisation.

Strengths and weaknesses

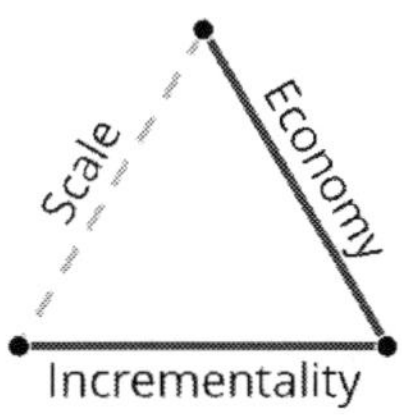

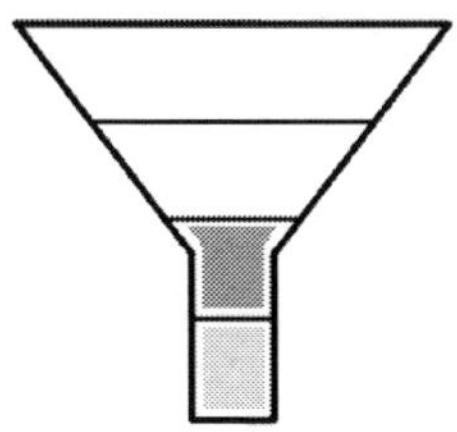

Closed-group performance is dictated by the **relevance** of your offer to the target audience.

You can influence this in several ways, including:

- Secure 'discovery' placements to help potential customers find you
- Secure regular email coverage to members

What do they offer?

Closed groups take the basic incentive concept and use it to drive a unique service. What closed groups really want to say is 'our offer is different from others on the market'.

Private reward platforms often work at a different pace from public, mass-market websites. While a public voucher code or cashback offer can deliver an instant 'sugar rush' of sales, closed groups are in less of a hurry. They are more motivated by member engagement, repeat usage and high-quality content.

A reasonable acceptance policy for closed-group reward sites

Closed groups are a great opportunity. Their members have chosen to use the platform, and they trust the quality of the reward and the integrity of the system. You should recruit as many such affiliates as possible.

Default PPC rule

- Do not drive traffic using PPC

Vouchers to promote

- Only promote voucher codes that are authorised for the affiliate channel

Affiliates to accept

- Any sale-positive closed group with an appropriate audience

Affiliates to consider

- Closed groups without a rule, presence in your country, region or territory

Affiliates to reject

- Not applicable

An unsafe cashback proposition

Imagine a merchant sells a SIM-only mobile contract that costs €10 per month. Affiliates can earn €10 (100% of the first month subscription) if they sell one. That is usually OK because customers generally renew their contracts for several months (the tenure).

That means a cashback site could offer the product for free. In other words, the customer would pay €10 and receive €10 cashback.

Would that customer, motivated by receiving a free product, behave in the same way as other customers? Would the potential tenure of that customer be affected?

At this point, the answer isn't certain - it could go either way. Let's take the example one step further.

What if a popular online forum, such as 'UKGreatDeals', promoted the deal with a headline like:

'Use this cashback hack to get a one-month mobile contract completely free - no obligation'?

Now, the answer is obvious: the value and tenure of customers who respond to that headline would be significantly different from that of others. The advertiser needs to plan carefully to make sure their cashback deals don't attract the 'wrong' sort of customer.

So... is incentivising bad, then?

Absolutely not! You just have to plan ahead, treat incentive affiliates and their members with respect, and protect your business from accidental loopholes.

9.5 Loyalty and reward publishers

Loyalty and reward affiliates offer benefits in the form of points, credit or discounts for closely managed groups of consumers.

What do loyalty and reward publishers do?
These reward sites use the commission they receive to fund benefits and reward loyalty.
Unqualified traffic | Decision stage

Loyalty and benefits schemes are private environments, so you can offer different propositions without worrying about them leaking to a wider audience.

Common applications include:

- Employee benefits
- Corporate social responsibility (CSR) schemes
- Supermarket loyalty schemes

Virtual currency and points

Reward affiliates often turn the commission you pay into an intangible reward with a different perceived value. For example, a €10 commission may turn into '2,000 points', with an equivalent cash value of €7.50.

Supermarket in-house reward schemes are a good example. The reward is turned into points that can be exchanged for their own goods and services. The perceived value of the reward encourages brand loyalty and repeat purchases.

This is a powerful and lucrative technique, and affiliates that offer it are great targets to recruit to your program. They tend to work with a curated selection of advertisers, so you may need to offer more than your normal proposition to qualify.

Working with reward and loyalty publishers

Strengths and weaknesses

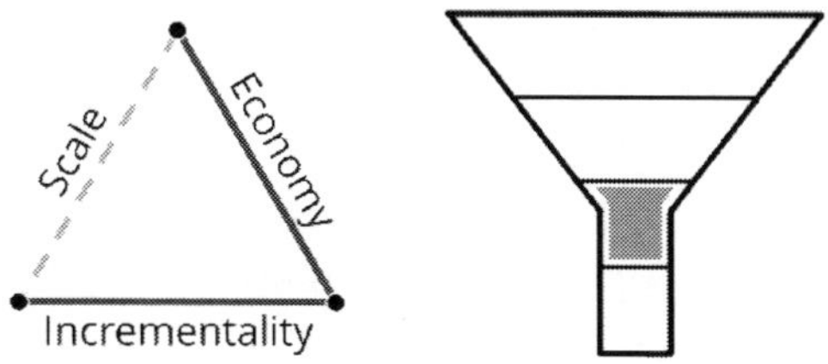

Participation in employee benefits schemes and other loyalty programs is usually negotiated individually, and providers of such schemes are often very selective about who they work with. They can deliver a lot of sales, but penetrating the whole market can take a long time.

You can influence this in several ways:

- Highlight the brand appeal of your company
- Add plenty of trust messaging to your website
- Offer more favourable commission rates

What do reward and loyalty affiliates value most?

Loyalty publishers use the same basic model as cashback websites, but the rewards they offer are more closely associated with their own reputation. They are looking for advertisers that enhance both their value proposition and service levels.

When recruiting such publishers to your affiliate program:

- Structure commission rates so loyalty affiliates can offer higher perceived value than public cashback sites
- Validate and pay commissions regularly and promptly
- Implement a fair and transparent transaction query policy

The best thing reward and loyalty affiliates can offer

Good loyalty partners challenge you to take advantage of this sandbox environment regularly by experimenting with different rewards and discounts. In return, they can make sure more potential customers see your offer.

It's not always about the commission

Affiliate marketing is not always the main source of income for loyalty services. In fact, some loyalty services don't care about the commission at all - they are simply looking for unique propositions for their members.

Consider exchanging some of the commission you pay for a strong discount code.

All programs allow you to change the commission rate for individual affiliates, and you can prevent the code being 'leaked' online by using your network's exclusive voucher code features.

A reasonable acceptance policy for closed-group reward sites

Closed groups are a great opportunity, particularly employee benefit schemes. Their members are loyal to the platform because it is an integral part of their employment. They trust the quality of the reward and the integrity of the system. You should recruit as many as possible.

Default PPC rule

- Do not drive traffic using PPC

Vouchers to promote

- Only promote voucher codes that are authorised for the affiliate channel

Affiliates to accept

- All genuine employee benefit websites

Affiliates to consider

- Any private loyalty service with a presence in your country, region or territory

Affiliates to reject

- Not applicable

Constructing a 'safe' reward proposition

How you describe incentive deals can make a big difference.

Consider this reward offer:

> **'Get a €30 gift card when you order an iPhone from widgets.com'**

You can understand what this means, but the wording could expose you to some risk.

There are several things you need to consider.

The product

Does the offer apply to all iPhones? That seems unlikely. There are many different phone models and ways to purchase, like SIM-free, pre-owned, upgrades or a new service contract. The commission for these categories is very different, ranging from €5 for SIM-free to €100+ for a new contract.

The action being rewarded

In this case, the stated action is 'when you order'. What if the order is never delivered or the customer returns the product? You can only reward a *valid, delivered purchase*. Usually, the word 'purchase' is a good choice, but this example is for a phone *contract*. The reward is triggered after the customer has *started* their new contract with the phone network and hasn't cancelled it after 28 days.

The reward

The reward is a €30 gift card, but where can you spend it?

Extra terms

Terms and conditions protect you if the order is cancelled while upholding the customer's statutory rights.

You don't have to include all these conditions in the offer's headline, but they must be presented somewhere.

Let's try again, taking the considerations above into account:

> **'Get a €30 Amazon voucher when you start a new iPhone 14 contract through widgets.com*'**
>
> *** Terms and conditions apply - click here for more details.**

The end result looks very similar, but a few simple changes have made the reward and the desired action much clearer, protecting you and the affiliate from misunderstandings and complaints.

9.6 Voucher sites

Voucher and coupon sites have evolved to form one of today's largest areas of affiliate marketing. They generate a lot of affiliate commissions and are often among the top-performing affiliates on a program.

What do voucher and coupon sites do?
Voucher sites collect and list voucher codes, coupons and offers for online retailers. They specialise in SEO and are often among the top search results for brand names.
Unqualified traffic | Decision / purchase stage

Discount code or voucher code?

The terms 'discount code, 'voucher code'and 'promo code' are used interchangeably in affiliate marketing. Since codes can be associated with benefits other than a discount this book will tend to call them 'voucher codes', but you will regularly find publishers using all three terms to describe any type of code.

Should I offer voucher codes?

Every e-commerce business has different costs and margins. I can't tell you if codes are right for you, but they can certainly be a significant source of sales and exposure.

It's important to remember that affiliates did not make voucher sites so popular - it's the public that drives their success. Hundreds of thousands of consumers actively search for voucher codes every day, so you should consider tapping into that demand.

At the end of the day, it comes down to a simple question: do you want more sales with slightly less profit margin?

Do voucher sites generate new customers?

Every affiliate manager has a different opinion on the value that voucher sites offer.

For: all coverage is good coverage

A well-thought-out voucher campaign can reach a new audience and help undecided customers to purchase from you.

Against: the benefit is not incremental

Some customers will search for a voucher code after deciding to purchase from you. They might even leave their shopping cart to search for a discount voucher.

Which view is right?

It is fair to say that the effects of a voucher campaign usually involve a combination of the trends mentioned above.

There are a few things you can do to stack the odds in your favour and give your codes the best chance of attracting new customers:

- Favour publishers that actively promote your offers to their audience
- If your network provides a tool to register and publish voucher codes, use it
- Analyse the 'lapse time' for customers who used a voucher code
- Publish codes with partners that actively promote or 'push' your codes out to their audience
- Make sure the voucher driven offer is within your means
- Keep things fresh with a mix of long-term and short-term codes
- Communicate new codes and promotions reliably and in a predictable, easy-to-understand format

But I don't/can't offer vouchers!

Even if you don't offer voucher codes or do not have that option on your network, you will receive many applications from voucher sites, and you can still work with them if you want to. The traffic they can send is valuable to you, and they are usually happy to promote generic deals, like free delivery or seasonal sales.

If this is your situation, a relatively conservative acceptance policy is advisable. Welcome proven voucher sites to the program but avoid low-traffic or new sites to avoid unnecessary risk.

Working with voucher publishers

Strengths and weaknesses

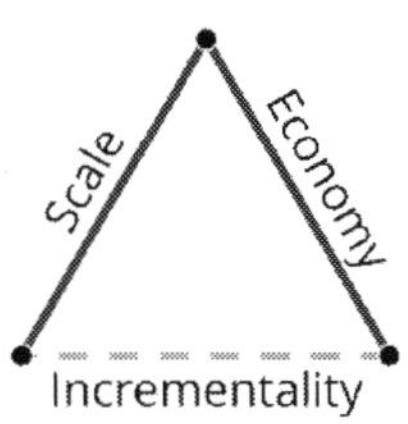

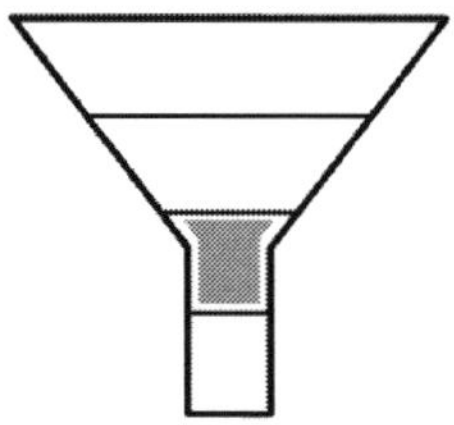

Voucher sites are hugely popular. Their default offering is built around SEO, and they work hard to appear when a consumer searches for 'yourbrand voucher codes'.

There are several ways you can influence the effectiveness of these sites for you:

- Choose how and when the voucher box appears in your checkout
- Secure regular email coverage to reach new people
- Offer voucher codes that favour or only work for new customers

Like cashback, the aim of vouchers is to reach people who may not have heard of your brand before. This extra coverage may come at the cost of increased commission or a tenancy payment, so you need to make sure it is within your means.

The most valuable thing a voucher site can offer

Why wait for consumers to search for voucher codes? What if you could send them straight to prospective customers?

As we have explained, voucher sites rely on inbound traffic, but the most popular ones can also reach out to their visitors. If you can convince a voucher site to feature your offer in an email, social post or push message, then you could be on to a winner.

What voucher affiliates value most

Voucher sites often look the same and promote the same vouchers and offers as their peers. Exclusive and unique offers help them stand out and offer real value to their visitors.

SEO considerations

SEO is fundamental for voucher sites. Many people search Google for terms like 'widgets.com voucher codes', so voucher sites compete fiercely to achieve the highest possible rank for that search term.

Unfortunately, they are also competing against you. A well-established voucher site could easily appear above you in a Google search for your own brand name.

What types of code can I offer?

Your e-commerce software will dictate the type of voucher code you can offer, but most will support the following types:

- Discount off the total price
- Fixed discount
- Free/discounted postage
- Free gift
- Discount for new customers

Codes with a discount

When most customers look for voucher codes, they are really thinking, 'I want to spend less'. Affiliates thrive off that demand, so vouchers with a discount will always be very popular.

Benefits

- Lots of natural demand
- Affiliates will always value these codes
- Supported by most e-commerce software

Discount codes can help you to 'hunt' for specific customers. Every discount you offer costs money, so you should try to get something out of it as well.

You may earn less profit on the sale, but you can achieve some of your other goals by rewarding the behaviour you want.

Here are some examples:

- Product category - '10% off all pool accessories'
- Specific product - '25% off the Miracle Tomato Planter'
- Minimum basket value - '10% off when you spend over €50'

Codes for free postage

'Free postage' is a common voucher offer. It doesn't usually cost you a fortune, but every customer can see the benefit. Though it may not seem very exciting, it can be very effective.

Benefits of postage codes

- Free postage codes can be great if you sell larger items with high delivery costs, which can discourage customers
- They help steer customers to your preferred/most cost-effective/most reliable postage method
- A free postage voucher code can discourage potential customers from searching further afield for a bigger discount - they have looked for a code, received something tangible and are satisfied

Even with free postage, there can be some risks. You can minimise these by:

- Introducing a minimum cost, such as 'Free delivery when you spend over €25'. The minimum spend should be reasonable – it is there to protect you from spending €5 to deliver a €2 order
- Making a separate, private code available to your most frequent customers - you don't have to pay commission when this code is used, and if affiliates promote it, they won't be rewarded

There is room for creativity with free postage. Consider this example:

> **'Use voucher code MOTHERSDAY634 for free delivery guaranteed to arrive by Saturday 26th March'**

This message is more powerful because it enriches a standard free postage offer with seasonal messaging and a sense of urgency. It has a potential cost-saving built into the promise of 'delivery by the 26th' - orders placed a week before that date won't require expensive courier delivery to arrive on time.

Communicating your voucher code effectively

- Ask your key affiliates what information they need and how they like to receive it
- Make the actual code short and easy to remember
- Make the description concise and catchy
- Use the official voucher tool in the network interface to register and distribute the codes
- Set a time limit to avoid confusion, especially for delivery-related offers
- Always communicate the code's start and expiry dates
- Make it clear if the offer dates are inclusive, like whether 'by 26th March' means the start or end of that day

Can I pay a different commission rate when a code is used?

In an ideal world, you should pay the same commission rate for every sale, regardless of whether a discount was applied. In practice, this may not be possible. The important thing is to be consistent and fair.

Most self-managed programs limit you to one commission group, which means you can't use the tracking on your site to affect the commission rate. Instead, you will need to change the rate for all sales through a particular affiliate.

Exclusive codes

Because of their desire to stand out from their rivals, voucher sites of all sizes regularly ask for an 'exclusive, market-leading' offer. This can be a potent tool, so make sure you use it wisely:

- Get as much proactive coverage as possible in return
- Synchronise it with key seasonal or peak trading times to make the most of demand
- Make sure the voucher code is tracked in the affiliate platform to monitor its performance

Most affiliate networks provide a way to restrict voucher codes to specific affiliates. Some platforms ensure other affiliates can't earn commission from specific codes, while others actively allocate the commission to the designated 'owner' of the code.

Like tenancy charges (discussed in chapter 11), exclusive partner specific discounts have become an integral part of the affiliate industry.

You don't have to accept every request, but don't automatically reject them either. View each request as a potential opportunity, especially if it is from a proven publisher.

Protect your brand

The voucher industry is very lucrative, and coupon sites are easy to build. As a result, every new affiliate program will receive dozens, even hundreds, of applications from voucher sites. However, many of these sites make very few sales or none at all.

If your chosen network has an indicator of past performance, then use it. For example, Awin lists an 'Awin Index' score that shows how the affiliate compares to other publishers.

Paid media rights are important to voucher sites

Only one site can appear at number one in a Google search for 'widgets.com vouchers', but anyone can bid on PPC to get instant results.

Voucher sites value this channel for earning commission, so you shouldn't give it away for free. Consider trading permission to use 'brand + voucher' PPC terms for something you value, such as inclusion in emails or social media coverage.

Reporting

Voucher code tracking

Most affiliate platforms allow you to record whether a specific voucher code has been used. This may require some extra work to adapt your tracking, but if you plan to offer voucher codes regularly, it is worth implementing.

Lapse times

Almost every affiliate order has a **lapse time**, which is simply the time difference between the affiliate click and when the sale occurred. It is usually measured in minutes.

A short lapse time - less than three minutes - indicates that the customer found the code and made a purchase very quickly. Longer intervals mean they took time to look around your site and choose a product.

How does the voucher code lapse time compare to other sales? A significant difference indicates that customers who arrived from a voucher website are behaving differently.

Policies

IAB code of conduct

For much of the 2010s, voucher sites were a hot topic in the affiliate industry. They were making huge amounts of money, and large sites were tempted to mislead customers to make even more sales.

In 2016, the IAB published a code of conduct to help encourage responsible behaviour, and many of the major networks signed up to it.

The code essentially ensures that:

- Affiliates don't trigger affiliate tracking when they shouldn't
- Affiliates don't make codes up
- Expired codes are marked properly
- The customer gets what they were expecting

In practice, the guidelines are hard to enforce and have fallen out of favour - they were last updated in June 2017 - but they are the only official guidance in circulation, and can still be effective is properly promoted.

The full code is located here:

ttps://www.iabuk.com/sites/default/files/IAB UK Voucher Code of Conduct V4.0 June 2017.docx

Concise IAB summary

The code of conduct is written in 'legal speak', which isn't easy to digest or understand quickly. To ensure your affiliates understand the rules, you can release a summary to accompany the official document.

If you publish voucher codes, you must follow the IAB code of conduct.

These rules apply to all voucher codes that work on our website, regardless of where the code came from:

- You are responsible for the accuracy and validity of all voucher codes, even if they were listed by your members or users
- Voucher listings should not try to mislead or 'trick' visitors into clicking your affiliate links
- Affiliate links cannot be opened in the background, in an iframe or using any other hidden method
- The visitor must know when they are sent to the advertiser's website
- Affiliate tracking should only be triggered when the visitor makes a positive action (i.e., clicking a link), knowing that this will display a voucher code and open the advertiser's website
- Please only display voucher codes that have been authorised for affiliate use
- Please do not list voucher codes that you know have been issued to another affiliate on an exclusive basis
- Make the key information about the voucher or offer immediately available and visible, including the start date, expiry date and accurate information about the discount
- Make extra terms and conditions for the voucher accessible on the page that the voucher or coupon is displayed on
- If the visitor clicks a link expecting a voucher code, they should receive a voucher code
- Expired vouchers should be clearly marked as such - simply showing the expiry date is not sufficient

A reasonable acceptance policy for voucher affiliates

The following policy is pretty middle of the road. It includes proven opportunities and excludes the long tail of lower-quality voucher sites. There is no correct or incorrect policy, but this is a fairly standard approach.

Default PPC rules

- Do not allow bidding on 'brand + voucher' terms.
- Permit brand bidding in return for extra promotion at key times - not always on.

Vouchers to promote

- Only promote voucher codes that are authorised for the affiliate channel

Affiliates to accept

- At least one large, established voucher site, which must have a rate card or media pack containing opportunities for you to use when appropriate

Affiliates to consider

- Sites that communicate with you and offer something proactive beyond their default listings

Affiliates to reject

- Template voucher sites with no USP
- Sites with no record of making sales in the past
- Sites which are under construction or well out of date
- Any site which is not IAB compliant (see below)

The click to reveal mechanism

Most voucher sites use a mechanism called **click to reveal**. This means the code is hidden until the visitor clicks on a special button or link.

Click to reveal is what makes voucher sites lucrative - when the visitor clicks to reveal the voucher code, they trigger an affiliate cookie. It also makes the sites very 'sticky' and explains why they generate so much commission.

Large voucher sites use a proven linking method that has been well vetted by the networks. Smaller or less scrupulous sites may bend the rules. If you spot unusual traffic patterns from a voucher affiliate, the first port of call is to check where and how your code is displayed - is the affiliate following the rules?

The voucher box in your checkout

When customers see the "enter a promo code" box in your checkout, they may start looking for voucher codes. They may leave your website to search for discounts on your social media accounts or Google.

You will never be able to completely stop this behaviour, but you can discourage it when there is no code available.

The easiest way is simply to hide the promo code box when it isn't required. Your e-commerce platforms may facilitate this with built-in options or through plugins.

9.7 Deal affiliates

Deals and discounts are a sure-fire way to make consumers think twice. Everyone loves a bargain, and a lot of consumers start their shopping journey by searching for 'cheap widgets' or 'widget offers'.

What do deal affiliates do?
Deal affiliates promote your offers, deals and promotions on their websites and social media accounts.
Unqualified traffic | Research / decision stage

The difference between deal sites and voucher sites

Isn't a discount or deal the same as a voucher code? Are they really a distinct group of affiliates? These are good questions. Indeed, mainstream deal websites are often indistinguishable from voucher sites.

However, affiliate marketing allows publishers to make their own decisions about defining a deal. They can identify something consumers value and focus on delivering it to them.

Examples include sites built around free delivery or free stuff. Or a site may focus on the best prices in one sector, like 'Latest RC Car Deals'.

While they may still publish voucher codes, deal publishers see codes as just one of several possible methods to help give consumers what they want.

Deal sites thrive around seasonal events

Big seasonal events generate lots of online searches for things like 'Black Friday offers' or 'Christmas deals', and deal sites are in an ideal position to fulfil those requests.

Working with deal publishers

Strengths and weaknesses

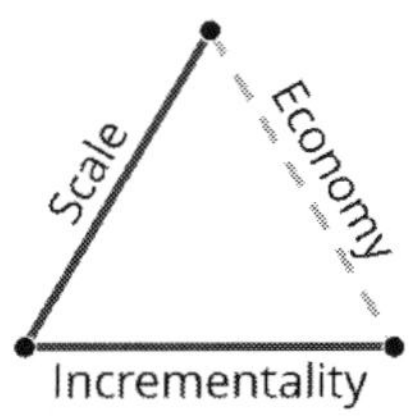

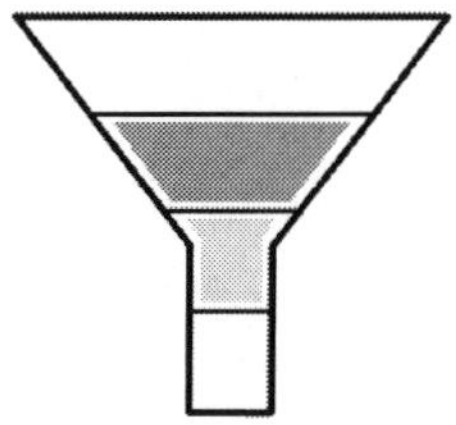

Like voucher sites, deal sites rely heavily on SEO, so a lot of their traffic comes from searches for 'yourbrand offers'. That in turn promotes orders with higher levels of discount and in turn less margin.

You can influence this by:

- Offset the discount by increasing incrementality - encouraging coverage on category and hub pages to attract new customers.
- Creating deals specifically for new customers
- Actively monitoring and managing deal affiliates - you can remove affiliates if their sales don't help hit your targets

What deal publishers value most

Deals and offers are hugely popular online and on social media. It is common practice for deal publishers to copy deals and offers from each other, making it very hard for them to stand out.

Exclusive and unique deals and offers help affiliates stand out and can be used strategically to promote a specific product at key times.

The best thing deal publishers can offer you

What you want from deal publishers is anything that actively reaches out to consumers. This could be email coverage, on-site exposure or paid advertising to boost social posts.

A reasonable acceptance policy for deal affiliates

This policy includes most sites with good traffic and engagement from their visitors. Partnering with unproven or 'thin' sites is discouraged.

Default PPC rule

- Do not drive traffic using PPC

Vouchers to promote

- Only promote voucher codes that are authorised for the affiliate channel

Affiliates to accept

- Established websites with proven traffic

Affiliates to consider

- Deal sites for specific groups of professions, like NHS staff

Affiliates to reject

- Template or low-quality websites with no USPs

9.8 Pay-Per-Click (PPC) affiliates

A lot of affiliates purchase traffic directly from search engines using PPC. Every affiliate program needs a well-thought-out PPC policy, especially if you intend to actively work with PPC affiliates.

What do PPC affiliates do?
PPC affiliates purchase ads that appear on major search engines when users search for specific keywords or phrases.
Direct traffic | Decision / purchase stage

Strictly speaking, PPC is the name of a payment model rather than a marketing channel. The term can be applied to any type of advertising where the advertiser only pays when a visitor clicks on their ad.

However, it is commonly used to describe paid media ads purchased from major search engines. The most popular PPC source is Google Ads.

Before we describe the two main types of media buyers, it is important to note that both have one thing in common - they are only successful if the commission they earn is more than what they have spent on the ad.

Direct linking

Direct PPC affiliates purchase ads and send the visitor directly to your website. The visitor usually believes the ad is an official ad for your brand - after all, it goes straight to your website and often includes your brand name or web address. Google Ads is the most popular platform, but services like Bing and Yahoo also generate traffic.

Arbitrage

Some affiliates actively purchase traffic to send to their own online properties in the hope that the traffic will generate more revenue than their ad spend. The landing page may be dedicated to your brand or present the user with a range of affiliate links.

Working with PPC publishers

Strengths and weaknesses

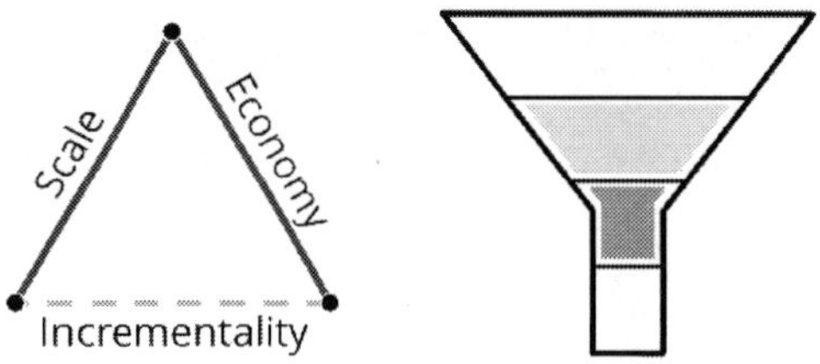

While PPC can deliver exceptional results, its weakness is *incrementality* because, by default, a lot of PPC affiliates focus on promoting your brand name.

You can influence this in several ways:

- Set sensible PPC restrictions for your program
- Form a close working relationship with your PPC affiliates
- Work with specially selected PPC partners that you trust

What do PPC affiliates value most?

Two types of keywords are very powerful:

Your brand name

You control access to your brand name, and it is up to you if you allow affiliates to bid on that term.

The brand or manufacturer name of your products

Some brands are very protective and restrict what their distributors can do. Generally, if you are not allowed to bid on your products' brand names, then neither are your affiliates.

Here are two examples:

- Most mobile phone networks don't allow their resellers or partners to bid on their names using PPC, a restriction that extends to their affiliates
- A well-known Danish building block toy is sold in many toy shops, but if you search online, you won't find any PPC ads for that product - from affiliates or the brand's own distributors

The best thing PPC affiliates can offer

PPC affiliates use their expertise and budget to represent you online. A strong partnership is one of **respect and transparency** in both directions.

With that in place, you should be confident that they are targeting your most valuable customers - people who have not purchased from you before.

Should I allow PPC?

If you don't use PPC yourself, working with a PPC affiliate could be smart. They spend money on the advertising, and you only pay for the results.

One advantage of paid media is that you can turn it off quite quickly. As long as you are working with reputable partners, you can test the water to see if it benefits your business.

A reasonable acceptance policy for PPC affiliates

In this case, there are no 'consider' or 'reject' rules - PPC rights should be negotiated individually.

Default PPC rule

- You may promote the brand using PPC with prior permission.

Vouchers to promote

- Only promote voucher codes that are authorised for the affiliate channel

Affiliates to accept

- Affiliates that fully inform you about their activity

Affiliates to consider

- Affiliates who operate PPC on platforms which you do not. Since they are not competing with your own ads there is little risk.

Affiliates to reject

- Affiliates who attempt to conceal their PPC activity.

PPC rules need to be communicated

You can't tell affiliates to follow the rules if you haven't made every effort to tell them what those rules are.

Your network should provide a simple way to specify what PPC affiliates can and can't do. If you have any requirements that aren't supported by your network, then you'll have to specifically include them in your program's terms and conditions.

For extra protection, consider adding a summary of your PPC rules to the welcome email sent to all new affiliates.

PPC rules need to be policed

Whatever rules you set; you need to be prepared to enforce them. The important thing is to make sure the rules you set are suitable for what you expect from PPC affiliates.

If you want PPC affiliates to contribute lots of sales, it isn't fair to overwhelm them with a long list of fiddly rules. The restrictions you set should be there for good reason.

Broad and negative matches

If a PPC ad shows in a search for 'brand.com special paint', it doesn't mean the affiliate was bidding on the term 'brand.com'. This could be a **broad match** for any search that includes the other words or phrases in the search, like 'paint' or 'special paint'.

You can avoid this by asking your affiliates to specify a **negative match** to ensure that PPC ads cannot appear when 'widgets.com' is part of the search.

9.9 Display and native advertising

Display advertising is one of the oldest types of online advertising, while 'native' is a new application designed for modern media owners. Together, they can help reach audiences who may not appreciate normal links.

What do display affiliates do?
Display affiliates purchase image-based or rich media ads that appear on websites, blogs, news services and other online properties.
Direct / unqualified traffic | Awareness / research stage

Display

Display advertising shows image banners to *cohorts* of users based on their location or browsing habits. Some display networks feature very basic targeting, while others can target a sophisticated array of attributes.

Display banners can be static images, animated or even interactive, with advanced html5 features.

Native

Native advertising is a recent development that helps content websites earn revenue by mimicking the look and feel of the website on which they appear. Native ads are often hard to distinguish from normal web content.

Is it PPC?

Display and native are paid media but are not considered to be PPC advertising.

While PPC advertising targets specific users based on the keyword or phrase they searched for, it is the visitor's location or browsing patterns that determine which rich media ads they are shown through display and native advertising.

Display ads are usually purchased on a CPM basis, but when affiliates do this on your behalf, they typically pay for the ads, and you pay commission on confirmed sales as usual.

Harder to monitor than PPC

While there are only a few major PPC search engines, there are hundreds of display networks in this market. It is much harder to find ads 'in the wild', so it is important to choose affiliates with good levels of transparency and communication.

A form of arbitrage

Display and native ads are purchased in advance. Affiliates hope the commission they receive will exceed their ad spend.

A well managed display campaign is **self funding**, regularly earning enough commission to pay for more ads.

Working with display and native publishers

Strengths and weaknesses

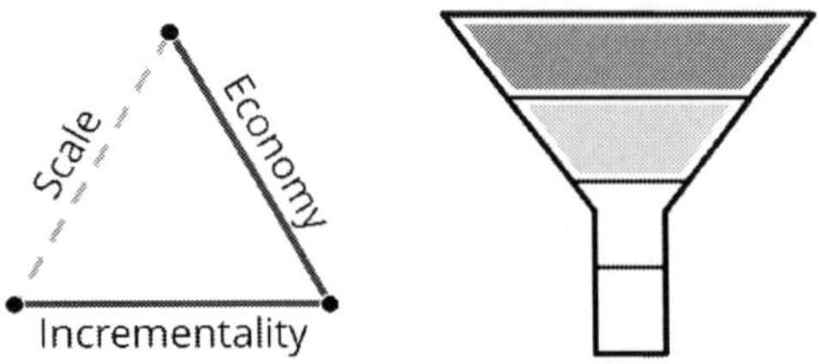

Display and native advertisers often use dynamic optimisation to make sure the host website is displaying the best-performing or most profitable ads. Competition is fierce, so scaling up can be a challenge.

You can influence scaling in several ways:

- Increase the CPA rate to allow more ads to be purchased
- Offer support to create high-performing creatives

What do display affiliates value most?

Display affiliates are practising a form of arbitrage, so cash flow is vital - you need to validate orders and pay your publishers as quickly as possible to make sure they can always afford to promote you.

The best thing display affiliates can offer

Display and native ads help reach the audience of websites that may not promote normal affiliate links. They can also target visitors who have already shown an interest in your product or topic.

Look for publishers who:

- Use premium display or native networks to place ads on quality websites
- Use advanced targeting to increase the relevance of their ad placements
- Actively optimise their ads for better performance
- Don't post misleading ads to solicit clicks

Should I work with display or native publishers?

Native advertising increases your reach and can place your brand on some very desirable websites. Even if you also pay for display ads yourself, it is unlikely to compete or increase the costs of your own efforts. Affiliate display and native activity can be a cost-effective way to increase your reach without an upfront cost.

If a publisher uses display or native advertising to drive traffic to their own website, there is very little you can do about it, but if they are active affiliates, you can use that relationship to make sure they respect your brand name and image.

Ad quality varies

Display and native ads are accessible and inexpensive, attracting a wide range of advertisers. Some will create well-crafted ads that respect your brand guidelines, while others may not.

You can always ask

Remember, you can always ask a publisher for examples of how they plan to promote you. It is up to you to decide if their response is accurate.

A reasonable acceptance policy for display affiliates

There is a lot of capacity and inventory available for display and native advertising. The following rules are designed to encourage any publisher that is prepared to represent you safely and fairly.

Default PPC rule

- Do not drive traffic using PPC

Vouchers to promote

- Only promote voucher codes that are authorised for the affiliate channel

Affiliates to accept

- Affiliates that fully inform you about their activity and/or provide examples

Affiliates to reject

- Affiliates that decline to explain how they intend to represent you online
- Publishers that use misleading copy in their ads

9.10 Comparison shopping services (CSS)

CSS is one of the newest types of promotion in the affiliate channel. It is an extension of PPC built around the features of Google Shopping.

What do CSS affiliates do?
CSS affiliates publish your products in the Google search results for relevant searches. The pay-per-performance model means you don't have to commit a budget to purchasing shopping ads from Google.
Unqualified / topic expert traffic | Research / decision stage

A new phenomenon

CSS came about following a 2017 EU antitrust regulation against Google. Aspects of the Google Shopping service were deemed anti-competitive, and the platform was obliged to allow third parties to list products in its general search results.

> 'Comparison Shopping Services (CSS) partners on the... platform doubled the revenue driven for advertisers across all verticals in 2021.' - *Message to Awin merchants, April 2022*

Since 2017, CSS has become one of the shining lights in the affiliate industry. It empowers you to place your products right at the start of a consumer's purchasing journey.

CSS requires cooperation

To get the best out of a CSS partnership, you should be fully informed about the affiliate's activity, and the publisher should understand your product range and specific business needs.

Most genuine CSS publishers will tell you that just picking up a product feed and launching ads without discussing the activity first is not the right approach.

The mobile industry is a good example. A phone contract has three possible prices - upfront cost, monthly cost and total cost of ownership - plus different storage variations, colours and contract lengths. Deciding the best value to use to use requires the merchant and publisher to work together.

Working with CSS publishers

Strengths and weaknesses

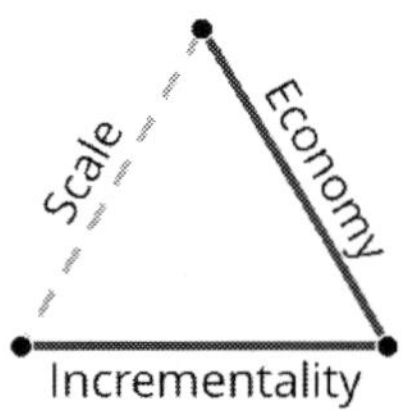

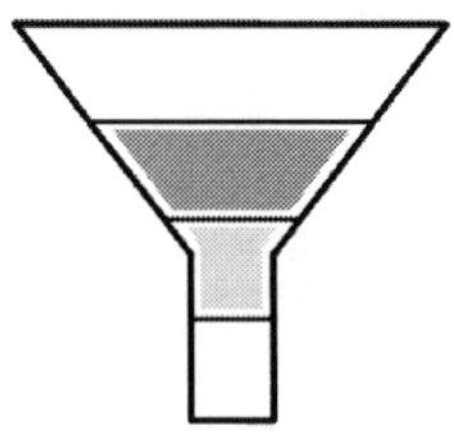

As CSS is a form of **arbitrage**, CSS partners invest time and money to promote you, so the limiting factor is usually the amount of coverage they are willing to purchase. Your CPA rate and conversion rate will dictate how much the CSS partner can invest while still making a profit.

You can affect the partnership by:

- Increasing the commission for the partner
- Optimising your feed to remove poorly performing products
- Focusing on top-performing categories and product ranges

What CSS affiliates value most

- Up-to-date and fully compliant CSS product feeds
- Accurate and up-to-date global trade item number (GTIN) information
- Sales and performance information to optimise campaigns

The best thing CSS affiliates can offer

These affiliates provide CSS coverage that reaches your competitors' traffic, not your own.

Can I operate a CSS campaign myself?

Only authorised CSS partners can bid for product positions on the Google home page. Don't worry; there are lots of approved providers out there.

CSS affiliates use product data

Product data is usually associated with comparison and content affiliates, but CSS partners also rely on it.

While they may be able to use your standard product feed, you will benefit from providing a dedicated feed just for CSS. This allows you to control what products are included and to tailor the information to suit your partner.

Dedicated feeds are easy to create. If you use an e-commerce platform, there is probably an inexpensive plug-in available to create the feed automatically. Your CSS provider may also provide a solution.

Unique identifiers (GTIN, EAN and Manufacturer Product numbers)

You must provide a unique reference - the GTIN - for every product you promote. In the UK and Europe, the unique identifier is called the EAN, and it is easy to find - it's the 13-digit number under the barcode on the packaging.

The GTIN helps Google to understand when different retailers are selling the same product. If you sell someone else's products, they probably already have GTINs - you just need to find out what they are.

Please note that Google uses GTINs to match products from several retailers you can't just make them up. On occasion the same product may have several GTINs. A good CSS partner or data provider will help identify the best GTIN to use.

How do CSS publishers get paid?

CSS publishers can be rewarded in a number of different ways, but as we are discussing CSS in the *affiliate* channel, we'll concentrate on CPA. Remember, CSS is a form of **arbitrage** - the publisher invests in the platform and pays to advertise on Google in the hope that the commissions exceed what they spent.

Think about what you include in your CSS feed

CSS results are influenced using sophisticated algorithms and bidding mechanics, but they are mainly driven by what consumers search for. If you have 20 products with similar names and keywords, it makes sense to present visitors with the ones you really want to sell.

This is why it is important to have a close relationship with your CSS provider - CSS campaigns are only really successful if everyone shares the same priorities.

Can I work with more than one CSS partner?

Multiple CSS partners can be useful when you are testing the waters. The Google platform will make sure each product is only listed once in a search, so there should be no conflicts.

Once you have identified the top-performing provider, it may be advantageous to work with them on an exclusive basis.

By consolidating your activity under one provider, you can take advantage of:

- An easier-to-manage relationship
- Economies of scale
- A single point of contact in the event of a problem
- More data to calculate conversion rates and ROI

Keep an eye out for changes

Shopping is an important part of Google's search product, so they update and improve the platform regularly. Your CSS partners should keep up with the latest developments, but it pays to be aware of potential opportunities yourself.

A reasonable acceptance policy for CSS affiliates

This policy permits CSS advertising without opening the gates to other types of paid advertising.

Default PPC rule

- You are permitted to drive traffic using the aspects of PPC related to CSS. Please do not drive traffic using non-CSS-related PPC (Google Ads).

Vouchers to promote

- Only promote voucher codes that are authorised for the affiliate channel

Affiliates to accept

- CSS partners that engage with you to discuss your requirements and goals

Affiliates to reject

- Partners that do not want to communicate or about your requirements

Top tip

There is also a free version of Google shopping that anyone can use.
It is a good idea to take advantage of this because it encourages you to complete the GTIN and product information for your products, putting you in a better position to provide the same information to affiliates.

9.11 Price comparison

As the name implies, price comparison sites help compare the price of goods and services from a range of retailers. Comparison sites are hugely influential, and consumer champions often tell consumers to make them their first port of call.

What do price comparison sites do?
Price comparison websites list similar deals together to help consumers make an informed decision about what to buy.
Topic expert / authority traffic | Research / decision stage

Comparison sites don't promote loyalty

Price comparison is one of the best sources of **conquest** customers - ones you gain from your competitors - but this works both ways. Most consumers use comparison sites to find the lowest price. This encourages switching between sellers, especially for regular purchases like mobile phones or broadband.

On the one hand, comparison may be actively helping your own customers to find a cheaper alternative, but on the other hand, they are helping you to gain conquest customers.

Don't let that put you off from using comparison sites. Your customers will still use them whether you are present or not. If you aren't represented at all, you won't have any chance to keep those customers.

Personal relationships go a long way

Comparison is a complex industry, and communication is essential. You will probably be given a point of contact or an account manager to help manage your presence and take advantage of extra opportunities.

Building a good relationship with your point of contact can make a real difference. A friendly account manager might let you know about opportunities first or be more flexible on tenancy payments.

Comparison relies on product feeds

Comparison sites rely on a database of prices that needs to be updated regularly. This information usually comes from a product feed.

Comparison sites can work with several types of product feed:

Network-generated feeds

Most comparison services can use your network's standard product feeds. Networks usually use a standard feed format, so the comparison partner doesn't have to reinvent the wheel to access your product data.

Custom format

A few partners request data in a custom format to fit into their system. If you use a plug-in or other software to generate your feeds, it should be easy to create a new custom feed.

A custom feed lets you do three things:

- Offer different columns and information
- Focus on a curated selection of products
- Include exclusive products or prices for a particular affiliate

Raw product data

Some sites may request access to your raw feeds - the same data you provide to the network to generate your feeds. This is usually to reduce latency – eliminating the network processing delay when you change a price.

As a rule, providing this data to trusted partners is OK, but be aware that it is less secure than offering it through the network.

Working with comparison publishers

Strengths and weaknesses

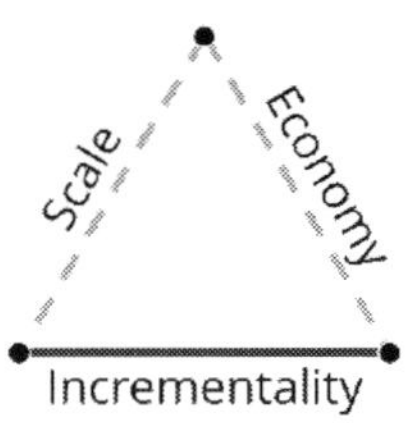

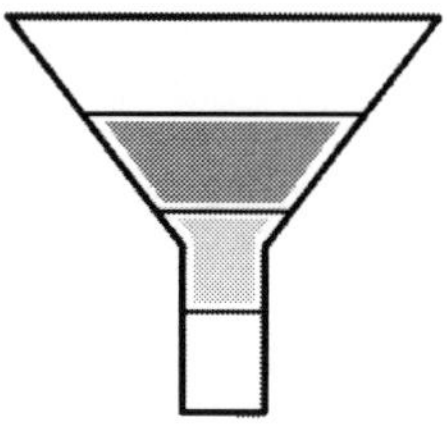

Wait, are there two weaknesses to this model? That isn't fair! There is a good reason for this, which really depends on your industry.

Comparison customers are usually prepared to select the service provider that best meets their requirements - usually the lowest price. That certainly ticks the 'incremental' box, but 'scale' or 'economy' depends on how many comparison services are active in your sector and what they charge for the best coverage.

You can affect this balance by:

- Negotiating a bespoke CPA rate that works for both parties
- Securing coverage outside the comparison service, such as email inclusions or featured placements

Comparison is usually industry specific

Comparison sites tend to focus on a single market or industry, like mobile contracts or home utilities. Services or products that need to be renewed regularly are popular because there is always demand for the best deal.

Tenancies are common

Most comparison sites have special featured or promoted slots to highlight particularly strong deals.

Securing access to those placements can be very lucrative. They allow you to catch the customer's attention *outside* the comparison experience, and you can make a lot of sales with the right product.

However, the cost of these slots varies a lot. Some sites only look for a good, attractive deal, while others may request an additional payment. In some industries, tenancy payments for placements can cost tens of thousands of pounds.

What comparison sites value most

Comparison partners will look for the following features to consider including you on their sites:

- **Price** - Are you competitive, and will your inclusion add value to the customer?
- **Availability** - Do you have enough stock to satisfy demand?
- **Credibility** - You don't have to be a huge brand, but is your site up to scratch, and is your business viable? Can the affiliate be confident you will still be around in six months' time?
- **Willingness to engage** - Are you ready to embrace comparison and all it entails? You don't have to accept every opportunity, but comparison sites are looking for partners that will offer exclusive deals and pay for more exposure when they can.

To receive the best coverage, comparison affiliates will look for:

- **Exclusivity** - Are the prices you offer to comparison partners available elsewhere?
- **Increased reward** - Can you pay enhanced commission or a tenancy payment?

The most valuable thing comparison sites can offer you

Comparison websites usually provide a linear experience. Results are presented in a list, with the most relevant offers at the top. To get the best results, your priorities should be **position** and **repetition**.

You can secure a better position either by ensuring you have the best prices or by negotiating for extra coverage *outside* the comparison listings. Featured or sponsored placements are usually placed at the top of the page.

You don't have to appear on a comparison page only once - different consumers value different things, so if you can be listed several times, you are increasing your chance of being relevant.

Top tip

Comparison sites often allow visitors to sort and filter their listings by price range. They may present visitors with options like 'between €25 and €45'. You can use this to your advantage.

You may not be able to offer the best price in the market, but perhaps you can offer the cheapest in the '€25-€45' category.

You are allowed to change your prices to compete...

If you are lucky enough to have a strong comparison presence in your industry, you will probably encounter competition from other retailers. Sometimes you will have the best prices; at other times, you may have to make some changes to earn the best positions.

There is nothing wrong with altering your prices as part of a strategy to get the most out of price comparison. This technique works best when the comparison site is expecting the change and they can offer better placements and coverage in return.

...But don't cheat

It can be tempting to change prices by just a fraction to look like the cheapest on the market.

However, affiliates find these artificial changes counterproductive and quickly develop strategies to counter disingenuous price changes.

If you aren't sure whether your pricing strategy will be welcomed, just ask your partner for their thoughts.

A reasonable acceptance policy for comparison sites

Comparison has few drawbacks, so this policy is very open. Accept as many partners as you can support and let the sales flow in!

Default PPC rule

- Do not drive traffic using PPC

Vouchers to promote

- Only promote voucher codes that are authorised for the affiliate channel

Affiliates to accept

- All relevant comparison websites

Affiliates to consider

- Comparison in related sectors - for example, a mobile phone comparison site may write content about mobile phone insurance or other technology products

9.12 Content sites

Content affiliates are the hardest type of publisher to classify, often including publishers whose activity doesn't fit into any other category. However, what they do can differ wildly.

Because they often rely on SEO, content affiliates are considered the safest publishers to work with. It is easy to visit their websites to review their content and make a decision based on quality and relevance.

What do content publishers do?
Content publishers create unique content that is monetised using affiliate links. They often specialise in SEO to drive traffic.
Topic expert / authority traffic | Awareness / research / decision stage

What types of content are there?

Content affiliates are hard to categorise, but these are a few of the things they can produce:

- Blogs
- Buyer's guides
- Product reviews
- Hobby sites
- SEO-driven content marketing sites
- Article repositories
- Vlogs
- eBooks

Content partners can supplement SEO

Every brand wants to appear at the top of Google searches, and it is harder to optimise for some keywords than others. This is where content affiliates can help.

Content publishers often have a strong SEO presence - even stronger than many e-commerce sites. When you are researching new keywords for your own SEO efforts, keep an eye out for affiliates that are already listed. They could help you to reach potential customers much more quickly.

Don't forget; the Google ranking algorithm is designed to reward the best content. Why wouldn't you want to be part of that?

Working with content affiliates

Strengths and weaknesses

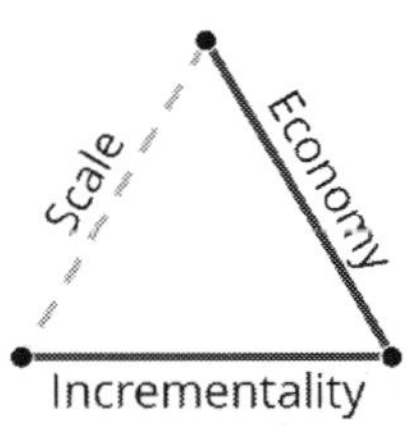

Content affiliates don't have the conversion rate advantages offered by voucher codes or the cashback model. Treated as a group, your content publishers may appear harder to optimise and scale up.

You can affect this by:

- Making voucher codes available to your content publishers
- Rewarding assisted sales
- Giving publishers advance notice of promotions, so they have time to create quality content

What content affiliates value most

Writing quality content takes time, so communicating **efficiently** is a must. Take the time to learn *how* the publisher likes to be contacted and what they value, then concentrate on delivering that.

The best thing content affiliates can offer

- Trusted recommendations and endorsements from an unbiased third party
- SEO coverage that your site may not be able to achieve

The last click model and assisted sales

We discussed the last click model in the tracking chapter. It rewards only the most recent affiliate to refer a customer.

As we have seen, visitors often search for cashback and voucher websites *after* they have decided to make a purchase. Content affiliates often feel short-changed by this because other affiliates may snatch their commission at the last minute.

That is where **assisted** sales come in - most affiliate networks enable you to reward partners that were involved in a sale but didn't refer the last click.

Evergreen content

A lot of online content is popular for a while and then loses traffic over time. Evergreen content is designed to stay relevant, attracting traffic and search rankings over a long period.

For example, an affiliate may maintain a page called **'Best Phone Contracts for August 2022'**. The URL stays the same, but the title and content will change every month, so it is always current.

It goes without saying that these pages are **very desirable**. Evergreen pages are a tremendous opportunity because they are a long-term proposition. Combined with content affiliates' strong SEO knowledge, they usually become more and more effective over time.

Content sites are often a side hustle

Many content publishers aren't at the stage where they can rely on their sites for a full-time income. Some might dream of the day when they can leave the rat race behind, while others may only see it as a hobby.

That doesn't mean they are less committed to their work or that you shouldn't partner with them.

It can be even a benefit - they are a source of authentic opinions that professional, full-time affiliates may not hold or have time to make available.

A reasonable acceptance policy for content affiliates

The terms below are designed to welcome as many content publishers as possible. Low-quality publishers are discouraged, while everyone else is more than welcome.

Default PPC rule

- Do not drive traffic using PPC

Vouchers to promote

- Only promote voucher codes that are authorised for the affiliate channel
- If possible, issue a dedicated voucher code for content publishers so they don't lose out to dedicated voucher publishers.

Affiliates to accept

- Publishers that maintain compelling evergreen content

Affiliates to consider

- Any affiliate whose content doesn't directly harm or conflict with your product or service

Affiliates to reject

- 'Thin' sites with no content at all
- Content that encourages undesirable consumer behaviour - for example, loopholes or fraud

Evaluating online content

As you research and recruit more affiliates, you are going to encounter lots of different online content. How do you decide what is valuable and useful? Let's ask the experts - Google assesses millions of pages every day, and they have released the details of three tests that they use to judge the quality of content.

While these tests are mainly used by Google to decide which pages are more valuable in their search rankings, they are a good point of reference when you are recruiting and supporting affiliates.

Beneficial purpose

Google guidelines state that 'websites and pages should be created to help users. It is OK if the purpose of a web page is to sell or promote a product as long as the page attempts to help and inform the user as they make the decision to buy.

If a page includes recommendations, features or editorial content, then it is considered to be helping the user. If, on the other hand, a page is just designed to drop an affiliate cookie without adding value, then it is considered poor content.

Beneficial purpose is desirable – content and advice that enrichers the visitors purchasing decision is likely to generate more engaged, happy customers.

Expertise, authoritativeness, trustworthiness (E-A-T)

Google wants to deliver the most relevant content for every search, but it also wants users to know they can trust its results. That is a sentiment you should share - editorial, adverts and recommendations from trusted sources are all effective in the long term.

The principles of E-A-T are communicated in the viewable content of a page, but some technical aspects play a part behind the scenes. Google supports special HTML meta tags and rich snippets that describe the content's author and their qualifications.

A page with a high E-A-T rating establishes its credentials through both content and structured data, such as meta tags, citations and open graph tags.

Your money or your life (YMYL)

Topics classified as YMYL are those that could have a negative impact on the quality of people's lives and/or their finances. This content is held to a higher standard to help protect users from poor or untrustworthy advice.

If a website or page is about a critical decision or purchase, such as health products, financial advice or an expensive purchase, then it is likely to be classified as YMYL.

YMYL topics include:

- News and current affairs
- Politics
- Finance
- Health, well-being and safety
- Shopping

If you feel that content about your product could be considered YMYL, it is even more important to consider the E-A-T principles and establish a beneficial purpose.

Look for potential affiliates with high levels of authority and consider what support you can offer to enhance their online content.

9.13 News and media

A lot of very popular online destinations are part of a wider network of websites and other channels. You could say these websites are the same as content sites, but their scale, reach and influence means they are worth discussing separately.

What do media owners do?
Media owners use affiliate links to monetise high-ranking content on influential and popular content websites.
Topic expert / authority traffic | Awareness / research / decision stage

Who are media owners?

Two things distinguish media owners from average content affiliates:

- They earn significant revenue from several sources, not just affiliate marketing
- They publish on more than one channel or website

Affiliates are just part of the marketing mix for these websites, which also feature display advertising, native ads and bespoke partnerships with big brands.

Haymarket Media and the Kelsey group are good examples. They publish established print magazines such as Grazia and Stuff Magazine, and also maintain popular supporting websites that extend the reach of the brand online.

They excel at SEO

Large, trusted sites have a head start when it comes to SEO, and they make the most of it by putting a lot of time and effort into their content.

They are proactive

News and media sites are always looking for the next opportunity. What are consumers searching for? What type of product do their readers buy? What is the next big thing?

When they identify a product to target, their first action is to create a page to establish an SEO presence. The page may not be 100% complete at this point, but the owners use it to test the waters and see if there is any traction before gradually developing and improving it.

It is worth keeping a close eye on the most relevant sites to spot these new pages early. When you do, you can contact them to say, 'I have the perfect product for you' and discuss partnership opportunities.

Media owners' recommendations are trusted

The best type of content is a review or recommendation, but online endorsements are often viewed with suspicion. Consumers find it easier to trust content and opinions from large, well-known websites.

They are capable of generating lots of sales

No, really - lots and lots of sales. With millions of visitors per week and relevant, evergreen content, large media owners can easily be the largest affiliates on any program.

How do these sites stay objective?

To avoid conflicts of interest, media owners typically keep their partnership and editorial teams separate.

Every publisher does it slightly differently, but a typical structure is that the commercial or partnership team compiles a list of products and offers while the editorial team chooses what to write about.

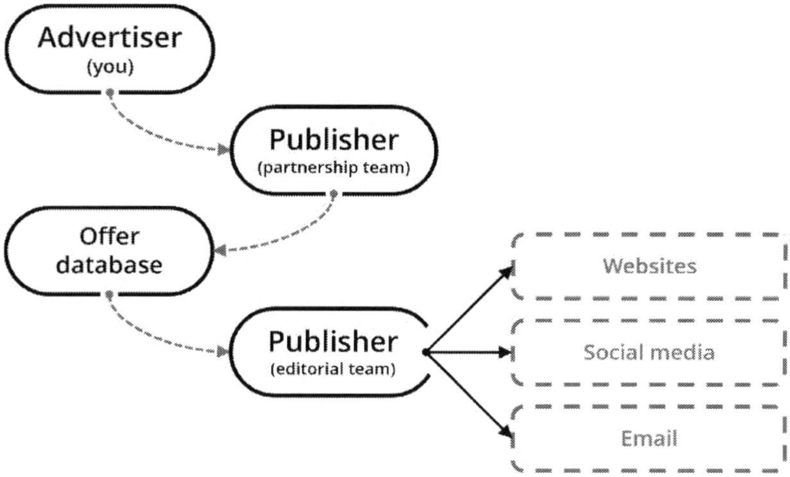

Other publishers make use of sub-network technology providers who specialise in adding affiliate links to organic content. Editorial staff are free to create hyperlinks to any product or website they choose, and the technology partner converts them to revenue generating affiliate links.

Working with media owners

Strengths and weaknesses

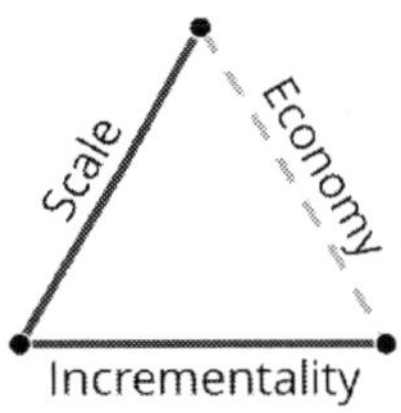

Media owners are very much in demand and often ask for increased rewards in exchange for their premium traffic.

You can affect this by:

- Monitoring the top sites for new opportunities
- Sending regular communications so that the sites always have the resources they need
- Considering tenancies or hybrid models for popular promotions, which may lower the cost per sale in the long run

What media owners value most

Timeliness and **relevance**. Media owners maintain a never-ending cycle of content creation and optimisation, so it's important to give them exactly **what** they need **when** they need it.

The best thing media owners can offer you

Frequency. While it's a great first step to be included or mentioned in a single piece of content, you really need to be featured regularly. It takes a lot of work from both parties to get to that point, but it is truly lucrative and worth the effort.

Brand names help

Large media owners design content to satisfy existing demand, so they often prefer well-known brand names. Your new affiliate program may not command a lot of brand recognition yet, but if you sell products from well-known manufacturers, make sure you highlight them.

Media owners thrive during peak periods

Every affiliate sees key events like Black Friday, Cyber Monday and the January sales as an opportunity, and large media owners are no exception.

As you would expect, they receive a lot of interest for these events, so it is important to be easy to work with. Make sure you fit around their schedule - some large sites may start planning Black Friday in August.

They won't be offended if you contact them

Some affiliates respond badly if you bombard them with communication, but large media owners are usually open to receiving relevant information on a regular basis. They may not act on every email you send them, but regularly providing well-thought-out offers and opportunities can help you slowly break into their thinking.

Keep the relevance high. Instead of a generic message like "We sell widgets and dongles - it would be great to work with you', look for proposals that directly address their requirements, such as 'We sell this product at €45, which is the lowest price on the market. It would be ideal for *this page*, and we pay a strong x% commission on sales…".

A reasonable acceptance policy for media owners

These are some of the most credible sites you can work with, so you should do everything you can to encourage partnership with them.

Default PPC rule

- Do not drive traffic using PPC

Vouchers to promote

- Only promote voucher codes that are authorised for the affiliate channel

Affiliates to accept

- As many large publishers as possible.

Affiliates to Reject

- Publications whose values or content may be objectionable to your audience.

9.14 Influencers and social media publishers

Influencers post use social media platforms to reach audiences and demographics that other channels may never penetrate. Influencer marketing happens when those influencers partner with brands for commercial gain.

What do influencers do?
Influencers create content for their chosen social platforms. They may feature products or brands in exchange for commission or tenancy payments.
Authority traffic | Awareness stage

Simply put, an influencer is someone who can influence others on a large scale. Their reach varies from a few hundred followers to millions, but they all work hard to build devoted and active social media followings.

Affiliate marketing rewards measurable results - that is, sales - while influencers like to be paid for ***brand exposure***. It is possible to combine the two, and a lot of influencers do publish affiliate links as a primary or secondary way to generate income.

There isn't a universal solution for working with influencers, but with proper preparation, almost any brand can benefit from an affiliation.

Choosing influencers

Marketers often talk about the 'three Rs of influencer marketing'. We're going to spice it up by adding an 'E' to the mix - RERR!

Reach

The reach is the size of the potential audience. Some influencers simply use their follower count, while others may add more detail, such as '1 million followers, 95,000 active daily views, 1,500 daily likes'.

Engagement

Reach describes the size of the potential audience, but engagement reflects how many people experience and interact with the content.

An influencer may have 1 million followers, but how many people see each post? Do they regularly view, share, comment and like the content? Most importantly, do they click attached links to learn more about the product?

Relevance

How relevant is the influencer to the product or service you want to promote?

Don't forget to think about the age of the audience - e-commerce usually requires a credit/debit card and delivery address, closing it off to influencers' younger followers.

Resonance

Resonance is the product of reach, relevance and engagement - it is the measure of how effective the placement is. The more a piece of content resonates with the audience, the more likely you are to get good results.

A good influencer provides enough information to show how their audience performs on the key points of reach, engagement and resonance. You need to decide how *relevant* that audience is to your product or service.

Working with influencers

Strengths and weaknesses

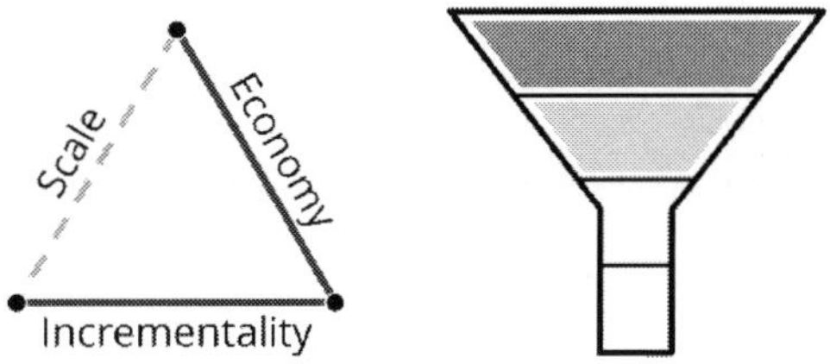

Influencers can reach huge audiences, but most of their followers may not be in the market for your product. That makes **scale** the hardest metric to control for these affiliates.

You can affect this by:

- Adding new goals to measure success, in addition to incremental sales
- Using assisted sales to reward the influencer fairly

What do influencers value most?

Every product or service that influencers endorse can enhance or damage their reputation, so **relevance** is essential to them. The best influencers always put their audience first.

When they enter into commercial agreements, influencers need to know they are being **rewarded fairly**:

- Consider a hybrid structure combining tenancy and CPA commissions
- Reward influencers by using assisted sales commissions

What is the best thing influencers can offer?

Influencer marketing reaches consumers at all stages of the purchasing journey. However, as we are looking at this from the point of view of your affiliate program, the most desirable features are **authority** and a **clear path to purchase**:

- Authority is relevance or affinity to the promoted product, so the recommendation holds weight
- A clear purchase path is a proven way to show affiliate links to their audience and encourage people to click them

Should I offer free products?

Influencers often have a poor reputation among marketers regarding free products. The general perception is that people become influencers just to get free stuff, leaving no way to generate a return on investment.

Your business will receive requests of this type, but probably not through your affiliate program. Things change when you start actively contacting influencers after you have researched them to establish they are worth working with, rather than a teenager with 17 followers.

A free product can form some or all of the payment for the coverage and equip the influencer to create unique content, like reviews or videos.

You probably won't meet the A-list through your network

Affiliate networks are not dedicated influencer platforms, and you are unlikely to meet authentic top-tier influencers through your network.

However, plenty of smaller social media accounts can deliver good results. If you do happen to meet a huge influencer, you can use your affiliate program to help monetise their activity.

Be realistic

Be realistic when you are considering influencers to approach. You probably won't be able to get Cristiano Ronaldo to promote you to all his followers, but that's OK. There is a massive ecosystem of more approachable partners to work with.

It's fine if you want to approach Cristiano as well - you never know - but don't build your strategy around his silky social skills until he has signed the contract.

A lot of named social media accounts are run by companies

Many of the social media accounts you see are no longer operated by the original influencer. In some cases, the face of the account never even existed, which is especially prevalent in the money-saving or frugal living niches.

While consumers may be disappointed to find this out, it is usually good news for marketers because it means these influencers are easy to contact, easy to work with and have well-defined methods to promote your products or services.

Including affiliate links in social content

Some social media platforms allow users to post affiliate links, while others make it harder. It is relatively easy to include affiliate links on YouTube, Instagram, Twitter and Facebook. TikTok and Snapchat make it harder, and it may be a challenge to see measurable returns from these platforms.

Exclusive voucher codes can help complete the loop. Simply give the social publisher a unique voucher code -when it is used, you will know the influencer was involved. Most networks can attribute sales to a specific affiliate using exclusive codes.

Marketing disclosure

Influencers are increasingly being cautioned to make sure advertisements, sponsored posts and affiliate links are clearly labelled.

You must make it clear to the influencers that understanding and following these rules is their responsibility.

You're the boss

Social media uses its own language and conventions, so you may need to be flexible, but you should still expect influencer affiliates to stick to the main rules of your program.

9.15 User-generated content (UGC)

User-generated content is written by your own visitors and customers on sites like online forums and review platforms.

What do UGC sites do?
User-generated content sites allow their members to publish thoughts, reviews, complaints and conversations about your brand.
Unqualified traffic | Awareness / research / decision stage

What UGC is out there?

- Review websites
- Topic-based forums
- Deal and bargain forums
- Voucher websites

Isn't this content risky?

Although UGC can appear quite toxic at times, it can also be a huge opportunity. When a community embraces a brand or offer, it can generate hundreds of sales in a very short time.

Your job is to:

- Keep your service professional to avoid PR disasters
- Avoid creating offers that could risk your business if misused
- Secure exposure for your best deals

Strengths and weaknesses

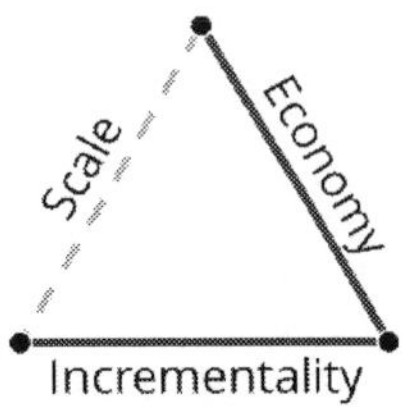

A lot of sales can be delivered by UGC, but the volume is notoriously hard to influence or control.

You can maximise the positive effect by:

- Focusing your efforts on platforms that you can influence and contribute to
- Engaging with the UGC platform when you can
- Using your competitors for inspiration - what do communities like or dislike about them?

Can I avoid being featured on UGC sites?

Sites that are monetised by affiliate links will often only feature brands for which they will be rewarded. You can control your presence on these sites by limiting who you invite or accept onto your affiliate program.

Other sites monetise their content using display, native ads or other paid media. They don't need your affiliate program to earn money and don't usually ask permission before allowing users to post about your brand.

Troublesome content rarely gets removed

UGC sites permit most things to be published as long as they are within the law. It is rare for content to be removed just because it is incorrect or not very flattering.

Review platforms

Managing your online reputation can be a tricky business. Most e-commerce websites have a presence on one or more review platforms, so it is important to choose the best platform for your online activity.

The most popular and trusted review platforms operate *outside* the affiliate channel.

Can I post my own content?

Most UGC sites discourage brands from from seeding deals or pretending to be a regular user to post their own offers.

However, Sites that rely on affiliate activity usually provide an official route for submitting offers or promotions. They may also offer to boost or promote coverage for an extra fee.

Every platform is different, but the first step is to open a line of communication to discuss your needs. It can take a while to be approved so it is a good idea to secure access to this facility *before* you need it.

A reasonable acceptance policy for UGC publishers

This policy is reasonably conservative, based on the principle that it is easier to relax the rules later than remove content already in the wild. Review-based websites are discouraged because it is often safer to use a review provider outside the affiliate industry.

Default PPC rule

- Do not drive traffic using PPC

Vouchers to promote

- Only promote voucher codes that are authorised for the affiliate channel

Affiliates to consider

- High-traffic sites that allow advertisers to submit deals

Affiliates to reject

- Review websites
- Content where 'is xxx a scam?' is the main sentiment or SEO keyword
- Sites that breach the IAB voucher code rules for triggering affiliate links

UGC is very fond of loopholes

A lot of the online communities built around consumer deals will happily discuss hacks or loopholes. Common examples include:

- Incorrect or accidental pricing
- Favourable cashback that significantly or completely discounts a product
- Voucher codes that aren't intended for widespread use
- Promotions intended for closed groups
- Ways to manipulate return periods and warranties
-

It's not possible to protect yourself 100% - that's why they're called loopholes - but you can do a few things to manage the risk:

- Follow the guidance in the cashback chapter of this book to make sure your incentives are safe
- Review all active voucher codes to understand which ones could cause issues
- Create enough deals and promotions that users don't need to find alternatives

9.16 Email affiliates

Affiliates don't have to promote you with a website. Email goes straight to potential customers and can reach millions of consumers in minutes. Email puts your brand or product in front of consumers before they have searched online.

What do email affiliates do?
Email affiliates send emails to their own distribution lists on your behalf. They may be solus emails dedicated to your brand or newsletters containing several brands.
Topic expert traffic | Awareness / research / decision stage

Types of email

Solus

A solus email is dedicated to your brand.

Multi-retailer

The most common type of affiliate email contains offers from multiple retailers.

Editorial

Editorial emails use affiliate links to support and monetise original content.

Working with email affiliates

Strengths and weaknesses

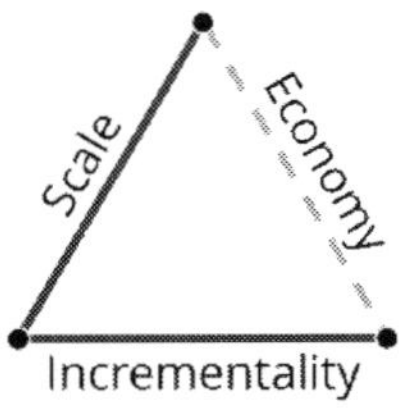

Email is a mass medium with good reach and reasonable costs. However, affiliates usually sell a certain number of emails over a set period, so once that agreement is used up, you will need to purchase or negotiate more.

You can affect this by:

- Entering into long-term commitments to reduce the cost
- Monitoring performance like a hawk to identify if the relationship is no longer profitable
- Optimising the email creative and landing pages to increase conversion

The best thing email affiliates can offer

Emails are personal communications that can reach consumers while they are working - on their lunch break, of course! - at home or otherwise not actively shopping.

Emails that include recommendations represent the most desirable type of content because they enrich your own sales message.

What email affiliates value most

Every time an email affiliate sends an email, it costs money and prompts some recipients to reach for the 'unsubscribe' button. Yes, sending an email can reduce the size of an email database. That means email publishers are always looking for high-quality content that their recipients will appreciate.

In their eyes, 'high quality' means:

- Strong offers that are easy to explain in an email
- Brand names that enhance their reputation with recipients
- Exclusivity

How are email lists built?

Email affiliates build their recipient lists in several different ways - some collect email addresses themselves, while others purchase details from other sources. The method used to build an email list can make a big difference to the conversion rate, as well as how the user feels about receiving it.

Does the email come from my brand or the affiliate?

As a rule, the recipient should understand that the email was sent *on your behalf* by a third party. However, you can't take that for granted.

If a consumer objects to receiving an email, it can cause reputational damage to everyone involved. That's why many affiliate programs stipulate that email content is approved before it is sent.

A reasonable acceptance policy for email affiliates

This policy is designed to expose you to safe opportunities and shield you from the dodgier end of the industry.

Default PPC rule

Do not drive traffic using PPC

Vouchers to promote

- Only promote voucher codes that are authorised for the affiliate channel

Affiliates to accept

- Affiliates that can demonstrate compliance with CANSPAM and email best practice

Affiliates to consider

- *Affiliates that can reasonably explain how they obtain their email subscribers*
- NB: These partners may be reluctant to share precise details - this is normal in the email industry because it is very competitive

Affiliates to reject

- Publishers that can't demonstrate or explain where their email list comes from

Safety and security

CANSPAM compliance

The Controlling the Assault of Non-Solicited Pornography and Marketing Act is a 2003 US federal regulation concerned with unsolicited emails - what we consider to be spam or junk email.

While the regulation originated in the US, it has become common for all legitimate marketers to insist on the basics of CANSPAM being followed. Everyone hates spam, so it isn't a hardship to follow the basic rules.

The recipient should always:

- Know who sent them an email
- Understand why they received the email
- Be confident that they gave their consent to receive the email
- Be able to unsubscribe from future communications
- Feel confident that their details won't be shared inappropriately

9.17 Sub-networks

Some affiliates operate sub-networks - you accept one publisher onto your program, and they distribute your link to their own network of publishers.

What do sub-networks do?

Sub-networks make your affiliate program available to their network of publishers. One sub-network can represent hundreds of sub-affiliates.

Topic expert / authority traffic | Awareness / research stage

There are several types of sub-network:

Technology/link rewriting

Services like SkimLinks and VigLink provide a snippet of code that turns any regular link on a page into an affiliate link, which is a very useful way to monetise forums and other UGC.

The largest providers provide an interface to manage your sub-affiliates but limit access to it- you may be charged for access, or it may only be available for larger partners.

Blog/content networks

Some publishers claim to provide links or deals to their own network of websites that wouldn't apply to your program individually. The promotion methods vary a lot, but banner ads are common.

Pseudo-networks

Some publishers repackage programs from other networks into their own offering, in effect pretending to be a complete affiliate network.

Blind networks

Blind sub-networks do not share the identity and activity of their sub-affiliates with their merchants. The lack of transparency means blind networks are usually considered the riskiest sub-network type. Blind sub-affiliates are often associated with unauthorised PPC and other paid media.

Working with sub-networks

Strengths and weaknesses

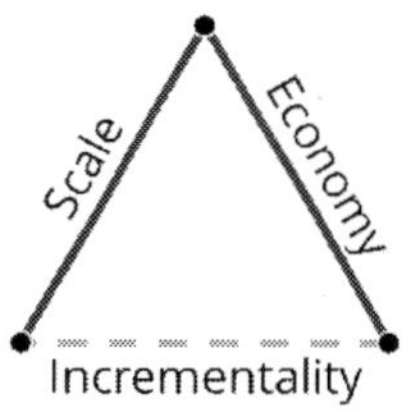

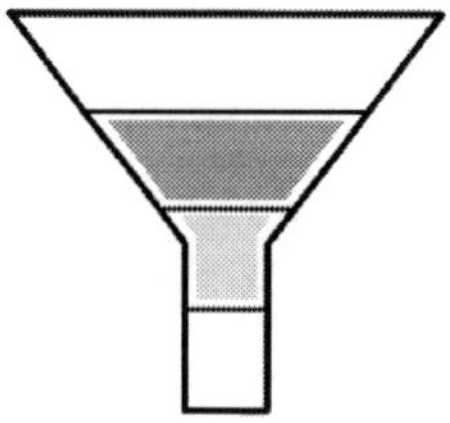

A lot of sub-affiliate traffic is based on your brand name, promoting it through PPC, native ads and other types of paid media.

You can influence this by

- Implementing and enforcing the sub-network code of conduct
- Actively monitoring search engines for unauthorised brand bidding
- Engaging with the tools the sub-network offers to review and reject publishers that don't add value

How much control do I have?

Each publisher is different, but the answer is usually less than with your primary network. You have a direct relationship with the owner of the sub-network (because they are your affiliate) but not their publishers.

Sample code of conduct

As sub-networks have become more influential, it has become necessary for companies to create terms and conditions to deal with their unique traffic. The following generic code of conduct is a good start. If affiliates follow these rules, you should be reasonably protected, and if they don't, you have grounds to remove them from the program.

If you have sub-affiliates or allow other affiliates to use your data, you must:

- Communicate all restrictions and rules of the affiliate programs to your members, including brand bidding and paid media restrictions
- Take active steps to ensure your members follow the rules
- Actively investigate unexpected spikes in traffic or sales
- Ensure that your tracking and redirection technology does not strip, overwrite or conceal essential information in the URL query string for your traffic

Sub-affiliates must:

- Ensure that traffic comes from a genuine, user-triggered click, where the visitor expects to be sent to the advertiser's website - tracking cookies may not be triggered in the background or within a paid media placement
- Provide information on landing pages and traffic generation methods upon request
- Adhere to affiliate program's restrictions on PPC and brand bidding
- Follow the rules of the paid media platforms they use, never concealing or masking content based on the referrer or similar
- Never use toolbars, browser plug-ins or similar software solutions to drive traffic
- Follow the UK IAB voucher code guidelines for voucher codes - https://www.iabuk.com/standards-guidelines/performance-marketing-advisory-group-code-conduct-vouchers
- Ensure that your ad-serving and redirection technology does not strip, overwrite or conceal essential information in the URL query string
- Cease any activity immediately on request

A reasonable acceptance policy for sub-networks

The aim here is to welcome as many partners as possible but to retain some control in the event of any issues and avoid the risks posed by blind sub-networks.

Default PPC rules

- Sub-affiliates may not promote the brand name, misspellings or variations.
- Sub-affiliates may not link directly to the advertiser's site from PPC ads.

Vouchers to promote

- Only promote voucher codes that are authorised for the affiliate channel

Affiliates to consider

- Technology/link rewriting services
- Sub-networks that respond to questions and explicitly say they agree to the sub-network code of conduct

Affiliates to reject

- Pseudo-networks that do not agree to the code of conduct
- Blind sub-networks

Sub-affiliates and paid media

Sub-networks are often used by partners that invest in paid media, such as PPC, display and native advertising.

Safety and security

Sub-networks usually provide the service they claim to and don't push the boundaries. However, a sub-network can be an easy place for individual bad affiliates to hide.

Sub-networks can be used to:

- Conceal unauthorised paid media activity
- Trigger affiliate cookies without sending the visitor to your website
- Help monetise malware
- Continue advertising a merchant after an affiliate has been removed from the main program

A lot of sub-networks offer a suite of tools to manage who can promote your brand or products, but they aren't always available to everyone. Some only allow their largest merchants to use them, while others charge for access. If you can get access to these tools, you really should.

How do I spot if something odd is going on?

There are three main numbers to keep track of:

- Clicks
- Sales
- Conversion rate

Clicks are usually the most telling indicator of suspicious sub-network activity -unauthorised behaviour is usually not very targeted and generates a lot of traffic with a poor conversion rate.

If the number of clicks increases suddenly, but sales remain static, it is worth investigating what caused the increase. Graphs are very useful in this instance because they make it very easy to identify spikes.

9.18 Technology partners

On-site technology enablers help improve your website's performance. A wide range of providers offer solutions promising to increase your conversion rate, offer strategic discounts and help visitors discover new products.

What do technology partners do?
Technology partners help you to add new or extended features to your website in one easy step.
Awareness / decision / purchase stage

On-site enablers

On-site technology partners usually introduce new features and abilities to your website. They use AI and rule-based engines to encourage product discovery and tactical discounts to help undecided customers to make a purchase.

What do on-site technology providers offer?

- Overlays/underlays
- Product recommendations
- Targeted discounts
- One-time discount codes
- ID verification - for students, NHS workers, etc.
- Content sharing

Off-site enablers

Some technology partners deliver their services away from your e-commerce website, usually involving contact or engagement with your visitors to prompt them to make a sale.

What do off-site technology partners offer?

- Cart abandonment solutions
- Retargeting visitors using display and PPC advertising
- Engagement emails
- Push notifications - mobile and desktop

Working with technology enablers

What does it cost?

Technology providers use all sorts of commercial models, but they are included in this book because they are often affiliates. That's right - they provide the service for free, and you pay commission when they refer a paying customer.

Will it displace other affiliates?

It is always good to think about how changes to your site could affect other partners. In this case, you need to ask, 'Will this feature steal commissions from other affiliates?'

If you're not sure, ask technology enablers to share the measures they take to preserve your affiliate relationships.

Soft clicks

Since technology solution is often installed on your own website, it has the potential to overwrite or replace existing affiliate tracking cookies.

Soft clicks are designed to help when there is a chance that a technology provider could claim commissions from other publishers.

Soft click tracking only creates a tracking cookie if no other affiliate cookie is present. If another publisher has already referred the visitor, they maintain the credit.

But I can do it myself...

Most of the features that technology providers offer can be done in-house. If you have the time and technical expertise to launch a certain feature, then great - that is worth looking into.

However, using a third party does have some advantages:

- Faster to deploy
- Less time spent on ongoing management
- Cheaper upfront cost
- Increased sales for your affiliate channel
- A second pair of eyes and fresh ideas

It's up to you whether you attempt to deploy a feature yourself or ask a third party to do it, but don't forget that every feature you launch yourself is an extra commitment to monitor and maintain.

A reasonable acceptance policy for technology enablers

You can't fill your affiliate account with technology providers, as that would slow down your website and confuse your users. The aim here is to select the *right* providers.

Default PPC rule

- Do not drive traffic using PPC

Vouchers to promote

- Only promote voucher codes that are authorised for the affiliate channel

Affiliates to consider

Consider solutions where:

- Your own e-commerce platform can't perform the service
- There are credible case studies and examples showing it works

> **Top tip**
>
> Some networks offer a master tag that is installed on every page of your website. It is a container tag, which means it can be used to quickly launch supported technology partners without adding any more code to your website.

Safety and security

Protect sensitive information

It is usually very easy to add a technology enabler to your website - simply add a small piece of JavaScript to your site, and you're good to go. However, these scripts often function by observing everything your visitors do and sending that information back to their servers. This can breach data protection and privacy laws if you're not careful.

Ensure the script doesn't accidentally pick up sensitive information, like payment details or personally identifiable information.

Terms and conditions

Most technology solutions communicate information from your own website back to a central server or database. This is not usually a problem, but you may need to update your terms and conditions or privacy policy to reflect this.

Ask your technology partner if you need to update your website's T&Cs or privacy policy to cover their service. They should

10: Regular processes

There are several key processes that keep your affiliate program running smoothly. These essential maintenance tasks make sure your affiliates are rewarded regularly and protect your business by ensuring you only pay commissions on valid sales.

Goals for this chapter
This chapter describes essential administrative and maintenance tasks you need to do to keep your affiliate program healthy. By the end of this chapter, you should be able to plan a validation process that regularly pays affiliates in a manner that is safe for your business.

This chapter will cover:

Assumptions

This chapter assumes that your affiliate program is fully operational and regularly making sales. You are now ready to perform essential admin tasks to make sure your affiliates are paid on time.

10.1 Validation process

Affiliates should only be paid when you tell the network that a sale was valid, so you need a validation process.

Goals for this section
This section will equip you to design and run the process that turns pending sales into approved affiliate commissions.

Why do I need to validate sales?

When an affiliate sale tracks, it is set to pending status. The validation process is the way you tell the network whether you are prepared to pay commission for that sale.

If you don't validate sales regularly, your publishers won't receive commission in a timely fashion.

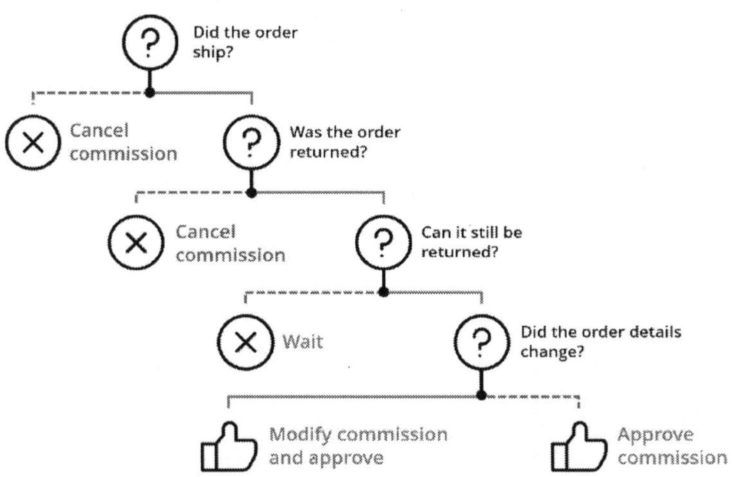

New responsibility
Validate your sales regularly.

Which sales should I approve?

You should approve sales that can no longer be returned or cancelled. In the eyes of your business, such orders are complete and can't be changed.

What can I cancel?

You should aim to be fair and consistent, but there are some situations where you will need to cancel the commission.

However, try not to think of this as a cancellation process - you should only decline commissions when it is strictly necessary, but you also shouldn't pay commission for transactions that don't meet the goals or spirit of your program.

CPS transactions

- Orders that were cancelled by the customer
- Orders that were never shipped
- Orders where delivery failed
- Orders that were returned
- Orders that were identified as fraud
- Orders that were obtained by breaking the rules of the program
- Duplicate orders with the same ID - allow one to track and cancel the rest

CPL transactions

- Leads obtained by breaking the rules of the affiliate program
- Duplicate leads with the same ID - allow one to track and cancel the rest

How do I tell the network?

There are two ways to approve or reject sales:

- Using an online form in your network interface
- Uploading a spreadsheet containing all your orders to your network

If you only have a few sales, the first option is fine. Once you start making a significant number of sales, it becomes inefficient.

> **Top tip**
>
> You should only pay commission on *valid* sales, so it is important to have a clear idea of what 'valid' means to you. Once you have that clear in your mind, write it down so you can concisely share it with your affiliates.

Auto-validation period

Most self-managed affiliate programs include an auto-validation period. After a pre-defined number of days, any sales you haven't expressly rejected will be automatically approved.

There are two things to be aware of:

- You might need to change the default auto-validation period
- If you don't check and validate transactions regularly, you could end up paying commissions for invalid sales.

Your customers' statutory rights mean they can return an item within 14 days of delivery. Most self-managed programs have a default period of 7 or 14 days, but taking into account weekends, postage delays, etc., an auto-validation period of at least 21 days is advisable. If you need longer, you will need to explain your reasons to your network, but they should agree if you do so clearly.

Payment times

Affiliate relationships work best when your partners are paid regularly. Even passive affiliates have cash flow issues, and paying them regularly is the best way to earn their trust.

If you hope to work with publishers that use *arbitrage*, then it is doubly important to pay them promptly. Cashback providers are also sensitive to payment times because they can only reward their members after you have paid them.

Most networks are able to pay affiliates every two weeks, provided they have validated their pending transactions and paid the bill for confirmed commissions.

A good basis for a healthy program

It may sound boring, but your approach to validations and publisher payments is a good indicator of how sound your affiliate program is.

If you and your affiliates are happy with the speed and quality of validations and payments, it usually means:

- Sales are being validated regularly and fairly
- Your network and affiliates are being paid regularly
- Affiliates can have confidence that they will be paid in the future
- You are more likely to be thought of as a reliable partner

Constructing an automated process

The validation process can take many forms, but it is often an Excel spreadsheet that analyses your sales data and applies some rules to decide if a commission should be paid. The aim is to assign every transaction the correct order status - confirmed or declined - as soon as it is safe to do so.

An automated process needs at least two resources:

- A list of all your pending commissions
- A list of all your shipped orders

All you need to do is match the transactions from the network with the corresponding sale from your system. If the order was shipped and not cancelled or returned, you need to pay the commission.

The main priorities of a good validation process are to be:

- Safe and fair
- Machine generated rather than manually entered, where possible
- Predictable, arriving at the same outcomes and decisions consistently
- Easy to maintain
- Portable across different devices
- Documented so different people can operate it if necessary
- Not 100% automated - this is your last chance to spot any mistakes, and a human eyeball can spot obvious issues that a computer will miss

Check for duplicates

Every sale you make has a unique order ID. If a user refreshes the order confirmation page or there is an error with your tracking code, the same order may track more than once. Some networks automatically remove duplicate sales, while others don't. You don’t want to pay multiple commissions for the same order, so you’ll need to cancel all but one of the duplicate sales.

10.2 Transaction queries

Sometimes affiliates may believe a merchant made an incorrect decision. Perhaps a commission was cancelled in error or didn't track at all. There are many reasons why a sale might not track, so networks provide a tool to resolve these claims.

Transaction queries (TQs) are used to address three types of issues:

- Querying the amount of commission being paid
- Requesting commission for a sale that didn't track at all
- Asking for a second opinion after a commission was declined

Self-managed programs tend not to use the deduplication and attribution techniques that cause a lot of TQs.

However, external factors, like security plug-ins, ad blockers and browser features, can still block affiliate tracking. You need to remain aware of the basics, just in case.

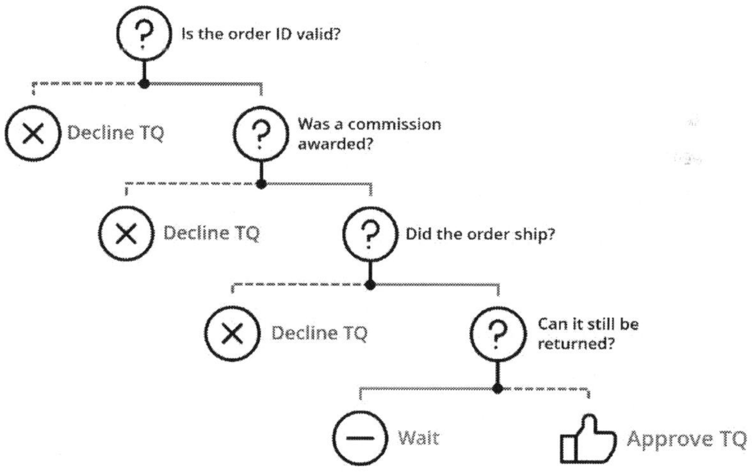

New responsibility
Review and investigate TQs regularly.

Who can submit TQs?

Any affiliate can use the TQ system, but it is safe to say some publishers submit more than others.

A substantial percentage of TQs come from cashback and incentive services, as they are best positioned to spot issues. Their members are incentivised to raise the alarm when something looks wrong, and are actively encouraged to flag any potential issues.

How does the system work?

Affiliate networks provide an automated way for affiliates to query transaction decisions and for merchants to respond. They use structured data files (.csv or xml format), and the results are automatically turned into commissions for the affiliate.

Approving TQs usually requires you to complete a CSV template with specific information before the system processes the queries automatically.

Some networks also offer a point-and-click interface to approve queries, which is useful if you only have a small amount of TQs.

Auto-validation

Transaction queries auto-approve after a certain amount of time, usually 60 or 90 days. This means you have to monitor and service your TQs regularly to avoid being forced to pay for them. Affiliates and cashback users have been known to submit fake claims just in case they auto-validate, so keep an eye out for that.

Goodwill payments

Sometimes a customer asks for cashback to be honoured when they aren't strictly entitled to it - a goodwill gesture to keep the customer happy. It is up to the individual account manager to decide how to respond.

Reasonable rules

Every TQ needs to be treated with respect and investigated, but that takes a lot of time. A few simple rules can significantly improve efficiency:

- Every TQ must have a valid order ID
- TQs can only be raised within 30 days of validation
- The order must be shipped, not returned and outside the return period

If a TQ doesn't meet these criteria, you can immediately decline it. The customer is welcome to re-submit if things change.

Reducing the number of TQs starts with your validation process

Your validation process is the point at which decisions are made, so it is also where you can affect the number of TQs you receive.

There are three reasons an affiliate raises a TQ:

- Something hasn't tracked at all
- They disagree with a decision you made
- You have been slow to validate sales

The second and third reasons are within your control. If you spot the same issue often, consider changing your validation rules so commissions don't get declined in the first place.

Are TQs open to abuse?

The most common reason for declined TQs is not fraud or dishonesty but simply an incorrect understanding of the rules. On occasion, though, TQ systems *do* get abused.

It is important to note that most of these abuses originate with the customer, not the affiliate. Here are the most common instances:

- Claiming cashback when they haven't used the cashback service
- Raising the same TQ with more than one cashback site to get paid twice
- Submitting TQs for commissions that have already been paid
- Submitting TQs for commissions that are still pending
- Raising TQs for order numbers that were simply found online (often on Trustpilot)
- Creating TQs for very old sales
- Repeatedly raising TQs that have already been rejected
- Claiming the wrong commission rate for an order - for example, a 'phone contract @ €40 commission' when the order was 'SIM-free phone @ €2.50 commission'
- Raising fake TQs for merchants that are known to ignore them (so they auto-validate)

Top tip

Spurious TQ claims are usually easy to spot if you investigate each claim thoroughly. Simply locate the order in your e-commerce platform and affiliate network, then check every detail carefully. The risk is not very high as long as you stay on top of things.

10.3 Reporting

You don't know how well a program is performing until you really look at the numbers. Every network has different reporting options, so here are some general tips on what to look for.

Short-term view

How many sales did you make today, yesterday or in the past week? Every affiliate manager should be able to answer these fundamental questions at the drop of a hat.

Online reporting is a great starting point - you don't have to download anything or open Excel, and most networks show you basic metrics on your affiliate dashboard.

Long-term view

When you look at performance over a longer period, it is easier to identify more lasting trends.

A long-term view is particularly useful to identify

- How much each type of affiliate contributes to your program
- Which affiliates are referring low-quality sales, with lots of returns or fraudulent orders
- Up and coming affiliates whose performance is steadily increasing

While you can see some of these things using online reporting, you may benefit from downloading the raw data from the network. This often contains extra information that isn't available online.

Transaction and validation dates

Most affiliate platforms allow you to create reports defined by two types of date - transaction and validation.

The **transaction date** is the default format for most reports. The transactions in the report are simply listed based on *when they happened*, which is ideal for looking at how your program is performing in real time.

If you create a report for '1st May-14th May', filtered by **transaction date**, you will see *all transactions* that occurred in that 14-day period.

Validation date criteria are more useful when you are looking at finance-related issues. Instead of looking at when a sale was made, it looks at when it was approved or declined. By their nature, reports ordered by validation date completely ignore any pending sales because they haven't yet been validated.

If you create a report for '1st May-14th May', filtered by **validation date**, you will see all affiliate commissions that *you approved or declined* in that 14-day period, regardless of when the sale happened.

11: Account management

Affiliate relationships are partnerships that take work to maintain and nurture.

Goals for this chapter

This chapter aims to assist in the ongoing management of your program. The strategies described should help grow relationships and encourage affiliates to drive more sales for your program.

This chapter will cover:

11.1 Values

Throughout this book, we have talked about treating your publishers fairly and respectfully. This starts with your policies and continues as your program grows and develops.

Goals for this section
This section aims to equip you with some general principles to bear in mind when you are managing your affiliate partners.

Assumptions

Your program has been live for several days or weeks. You are now ready to take your program to the next level by actively managing your publishers to drive more traffic and sales for your business.

Be transparent

Trust is crucial in building a relationship with your affiliates. Affiliates are unlikely to engage if they aren't confident in your proposition.

Be clear and transparent from the beginning to avoid misunderstandings and establish yourself as a trustworthy and dependable partner.

Transparency starts with your online profile:

- Complete every chapter of your network profile
- View your profile using an affiliate account so you understand what your publishers see
- Describe the steps you are taking to run a safe, honest and equitable affiliate program

Be reliable

The nuts and bolts of your affiliate program should work smoothly. Conversations with your partners should be about exploring new opportunities, not admin issues.

- Validate commissions regularly and consistently
- Engage with the TQ system to resolve issues promptly
- Explain your commission structure clearly and concisely
- Address technical issues promptly
- Check resources such as product feeds regularly

Be approachable

Publishers are very independent, but that doesn't mean you should recruit them and leave them to it. If they feel ignored or abandoned, their engagement with your program will decline.

- Make sure affiliates know who is responsible for your affiliate program
- Hide irrelevant details, like the finance contact
- Find out how your top affiliates like to be contacted
- Provide direct contact details for your top partners

Keep the relationship mutually beneficial

Affiliate marketing is about rewarding your publishers for a job well done. Your program terms should present a real opportunity for your affiliates to earn revenue.

- Accept applications from publishers whose goals align with your brand
- Set fair commission rates
- Be sure to reward all transactions
- Analyse your competitors to see how you compare
- Prioritise affiliates with whom you can build a deeper relationship

11.2 Super affiliates and the 80:20 rule

Your list of top-performing publishers is likely to be dominated by super affiliates - 80% of your sales could come from just 20% of your affiliates.

Every network has a group of super affiliates with the ability to become the top publisher for almost any program they promote. Super affiliates earn huge amounts of commission every month, and each one has the potential to refer a significant percentage of your affiliate sales.

The good news is that there isn't a special trick to attracting super affiliates. All you need is a well-thought-out, well-run program that is relevant and rewards affiliates well.

Super affiliates are always in demand and can afford to be picky about who they work with. To keep the relationship healthy, you must provide a steady diet of promotions with attractive commissions and conversion rates.

Is it always 80:20?

These figures represent a general rule. The exact proportion depends on your industry, commission rates and program policies. If you don't work with traditionally strong performers, like cashback or voucher sites, then the 80:20 rule may not hold true for you.

Some affiliates are more equal than others

This book is about doing the best job for all your publishers, but you don't have to treat them all perfectly equally. Super affiliates present a bigger opportunity, so it is perfectly understandable to put more time and effort into managing them.

If 80% of your results come from 20% of your partners, you should spend *more* than 20% of your time supporting and developing those relationships. It is vital to make sure your best partners are never confused about your program or lack the resources they need to promote you.

On a practical level, you should regularly interact with these affiliates with more personalised communications, responding promptly to their questions, concerns and proposals. A super affiliate should know that you will be there for them when they need you.

Super affiliates are likely to ask for tenancy payments or offer a rate card of extra coverage options. You don't have to take up every offer, but you should give each one due consideration and engage with the affiliate about them.

Most importantly, **let your super affiliates know** that they can rely on your support, assistance and encouragement.

Sutton's law

When renowned money man - that is, bank robber - Willie Sutton was asked why he robbed banks, he replied 'because that's where the money is'*.

The marketing industry gravitates towards super affiliates for the same reason. They are a known quantity, and excellent results are possible and achievable.

* This may or may not be true, but it's a good story...

11.3 Commission strategies

In the 'Creating your program' chapter, we discussed the standard or default proposition. It is worth remembering that you will have to step outside that as your program develops.

Goals for this section
After completing this section, you should be comfortable with the concept of increasing commissions to reward and encourage specific behaviour from affiliates.

Successful affiliate programs all come with a compromise

To make a truly beneficial partnership, both sides will need to give a little ground in what they expect from each other.

There are two levels to the compromise you will be expected to make:

Pay more

This is the obvious step - after all, your job as a merchant is to get the affiliate to try harder, and their job is to get you to pay more.

Permit coverage you wouldn't normally allow

This might mean allowing cashback, PPC or voucher activity when you wouldn't usually, or issuing bespoke deals or promotions for specific partners. The Internet rewards uniqueness, so this gives the chosen affiliate a powerful advantage.

The second level is where the action happens in affiliate marketing, so you will come under pressure to get there as quickly as possible. It can be lucrative and worthwhile if you are careful about the compromises you make.

As long as there is a clear path to making sales, you should seriously consider requests for bespoke terms. They are a positive step forward in your relationship with the publisher, and should make negotiations easier next time round.

Reward the behaviour you are seeking

The best commission strategies directly reward the goals of your program. If you want more sales, commission tiers reward affiliates for driving more orders. If you would like to increase the average order value, a CPA rate linked to the order value will help customers decide to spend more.

Common methods

Affiliate-specific increases

You don't have to treat all your affiliates the same. Super affiliates may request higher commission rates to launch your program or in return for extra exposure.

While self-managed programs come with some commission restrictions, they all allow you to offer different affiliates bespoke commission rates.

Transaction-based commission

Increasing the commission according to order value is especially powerful for cashback partners and can lead to a direct increase in the value of your customers' orders. For example, if your average order value is €65, offering increased cashback for orders over €100 could deliver real value for your business.

This is quite an advanced technique, and depending on your affiliate network, you may have to implement it manually as part of your validation process. Nevertheless, its benefits could be worth the extra effort.

Commission tiers

Tiers allow you to increase how much affiliates receive when they meet certain targets. A well-thought-out tier system safeguards your bottom line while encouraging what you really want - more sales.

Commission tiers can revolutionise how much your affiliates earn. However, they rely on the affiliate hitting performance targets. If a publisher usually charges tenancies, which are not linked to performance, they may be reluctant to accept a tier-based system instead.

Top tip

Bespoke terms and commission rates are not optional - they are an essential part of growing and optimising your affiliate program. Every successful affiliate program has made some sort of compromise to attract top publishers and encourage performance.

What should I ask for?

The coverage you ask for should enhance and supplement the affiliate's default proposition. For example, cashback and voucher websites are already popular with people who know who you are, so additional coverage should try to introduce you to new consumers.

Some of the things you could ask for include:

- Coverage on the affiliate's homepage
- Featured retailer status
- Coverage on category or hub pages
- Push notifications via apps or social media
- Inclusion in emails

Should I negotiate permanent or time-limited increases?

You can choose to step outside your default proposition on a permanent or temporary basis. Permanent partnerships show the affiliate you are serious, while temporary arrangements help you to stay flexible.

When to agree permanent increases

- To secure premium advertisers, who may only be prepared to work with you in exchange for an enhanced reward
- As an alternative to paying ongoing tenancy fees

When to use temporary agreements

- If the coverage you receive in return has an expiry date or supports a specific promotion, period or seasonal event
- As a trial while you are still getting to know an affiliate

Monitor the results

There is no such thing as a sure bet in affiliates. You should always keep track of the results to make sure you are happy with the outcome.

Affiliates don't set out to break their promises, but it is easy for things to fall by the wayside if different teams are working on your partnership.

- Make sure any extra coverage, placements or communications that you negotiated are delivered
- Closely monitor clicks and traffic to determine whether the activity delivered an increase

If you agree to a commission increase to drive more traffic and sales, *watch the results carefully*. Success or failure to deliver these goals will dictate whether you repeat the same type of deal in the future.

11.4 Tenancies

Affiliate marketing thrives on the CPA model. However, some publishers may ask for a fixed or tenancy payment to secure certain coverage.

Goals for this section
This section aims to explain why affiliates charge tenancies and to help you decide if and when they are appropriate for your program.

While affiliate marketing is built on the foundation of the CPA model, it is also common for publishers to charge additional fees for some coverage. These tenancy charges are often significant, so it is essential to consider all the pros and cons before you commit to paying them.

An integral part of the affiliate industry

While the use of tenancy payments divides opinion, the modern affiliate industry is built around them. They are a key tool for many publishers and agencies and are often the only way for you to secure the best placements and coverage.

With that in mind, it is important not to adopt the attitude of 'we never pay tenancies' or 'we have no budget'. Your new affiliate program might not be ready for them yet, but that could change in the future.

If affiliates think you will *never* want to engage with their commercial model, they will be more reluctant to work with you.

Why do affiliates ask for tenancies?

- Demand outstrips supply
- They want to protect their ROI from unproven advertisers
- The standard commission is too low
- The coverage they offer - like paid media - costs money to deliver

Ask the right questions

Good affiliates usually provide a media pack describing the coverage included in the tenancy package. A good information pack might include:

- User demographics
- Details about how the affiliate generates traffic
- Details of the extra coverage, how much traffic the affiliate typically receives and how much traffic they generate for advertisers
- Case studies and examples of past tenancy placements and the results they drove

With that information in hand, you need ask yourself whether your product or service suitable for this affiliate's audience. While affiliates regularly surprise advertisers with their performance, you should also trust your gut. A tenancy should be a calculated risk, not a gamble.

What if it doesn't work?

Tenancy payments secure coverage, not results. You can't ask for a refund if you didn't get the results you were hoping for.

Don't forget the override

The network override also applies to tenancy payments. If you pay a €1,000 tenancy through your network, you will also be charged an additional override - usually 30%.

Should I pay tenancies?

Many affiliate programs use tenancies regularly, but these tend to be established programs with large budgets. Self-managed programs may find it harder to justify paying tenancies due to the cost and the performance required to make them a success.

It is usually safer to enter a tenancy agreement to enhance the performance of an affiliate you already have a close relationship with than it is to pay a tenancy to a brand-new partner. An affiliate should be able to demonstrate that they can provide consistent performance with their *default proposition* before you consider tenancies.

At the end of the day, you can only do the best you can with the resources you have available. There *is* a tenancy package out there that will work for you, but there are a lot that won't. Wait for the right opportunity before you take the plunge.

New responsibility

When you do agree to pay tenancies, make sure they are paid promptly. The publisher may ask you to sign an insertion order (IO), which usually includes a payment schedule.

11.5 Activating affiliates

Some affiliates will start promoting you straight away, while others need more convincing, making activation an important part of program management.

Goals for this section
Upon completing this section, you should understand the difference between enrolled and active affiliates, why some publishers don't become active straight away, and how to convince them to actively promote your program.

Affiliates can fall into several categories based on their activity.

Enrolled - no coverage

An **enrolled** publisher is a member of your affiliate program that has not yet made any attempt to promote your affiliate links.

Active - no results

An **active** publisher is a member of your affiliate program and has published your affiliate links, but they are not referring any clicks or sales.

Click active

Click active publishers are members of your program that are sending traffic through their affiliate links.

Sale active

A member of your program whose traffic is successfully converting into paying customers is **sales active**.

Lapsed

A **lapsed** publisher has generated traffic or sales in the past but is not currently doing so.

New responsibility
Regularly review and contact inactive affiliates to persuade them to become active.

How do I activate publishers?

Activation is the process of convincing inactive and lapsed publishers to actively promote your brand.

Approve affiliate applications regularly (daily)

Affiliates often apply for a program to fulfil an immediate need - for example, to monetise some content or take advantage of a seasonal event. You need to approve applications regularly to make sure you don’t miss new partnership opportunities.

Auto-approve applications

Auto-approval removes all friction from the enrolment process. Affiliates can simply click a button to join your program and start promoting you straight away.

While there are many good reasons to approve applications to your program manually, auto-approval certainly helps

Prioritise promising publishers

You don't have to treat every inactive affiliate the same way. If there is a publisher you believe would be particularly effective for your program, contact them directly with a personalised message offering more support and cooperation.

Offer an activation incentive

Different affiliates value different types of incentives, so you could either choose an incentive that suits your preferred affiliate type or offer bespoke incentives to different publishers. An activation incentive could be:

- A bonus after the first sale has been achieved
- A bonus or commission increase after x sales have been achieved
- Increased commission for a set period
- Access to products for review
- Exclusive voucher codes

Customise the welcome email

Most affiliate networks send a welcome message when a publisher joins your program. The default message is usually very simple and can easily be improved.

Consider including:

- The affiliate's default tracking link
- Details about the activation incentive
- Top-performing products
- Information about your product feed
- Information relevant to the consumer - return periods, delivery charges, identification requirements *etc.*
- An overview of the commission levels
- Direct contact information

Send regular communications

Regular newsletters help keep your program prominent in the publisher's mind and should include promotions or content that the they and their audience will find compelling.

Activation continues past the first sale

Even successful affiliates can often do more. Think of your activation campaign as an ongoing effort to help *all* your publishers reach their maximum potential.

Can I remove inactive affiliates?

Inactive or dormant affiliates usually outnumber sale active affiliates - it is not unusual for 90% of a program's affiliates to be inactive and generate no clicks or sales.

It can be tempting to remove inactive affiliates now and again to make the account easier to manage and make your partner base look more engaged. However, there are a lot of great reasons to keep inactive affiliates in your program.

They have already shown an interest in your business

They may not be promoting you yet, but inactive publishers have expressed an interest in your business. You have their contact details, so treat them as recruitment prospects and get in touch.

They could be active using another account

Affiliates with large websites or portfolios often spread their activity across several accounts. They may not be making sales through a specific account on your network, but they may be using it to receive your communications, so removing them could lead to less coverage in the future.

Something is broken

There could be a simple reason you are seeing no clicks or sales - the system's not tracking them! Affiliate links are easy to break and just as easy to fix.

Your program fell short

Perhaps they did want to promote you, but something about your program doesn't meet their requirements. They might need specific information in the product feed or a resource that you haven't given them yet.

Your program is not the problem

Publishers often need several advertisers to participate before they start some activity. Some programs take months to approve new affiliates, so you may need to wait for everyone else to catch up.

You're on the list...

Every affiliate has hundreds of ideas for their next campaign or website. They will get around to it one day - promise!

In most of these cases, the appropriate response is to **contact the publisher**. Start a conversation, offer your assistance and try to remove the barrier preventing them from driving clicks and sales to your program.

So I shouldn't remove anyone from my program?

You can remove any affiliate from your program at your discretion, but activity status alone is not the best reason to do it.

Review your list of inactive affiliates, and consider removing them if

- You have exhausted all options in trying to activate them
- You have looked at their website/activity and are not happy with the quality
- You don't believe they ever intend to promote you
- They joined your program for something that isn't in your interest, such as promoting your competitors

11.6 Black Friday and other seasonal events

The first Friday after US Thanksgiving, or **Black Friday**, is the year's biggest shopping event. The affiliate industry shifts into high gear to meet consumers' ever-increasing demand for unbeatable bargains.

We will concentrate on Black Friday because it is the largest shopping day of the year, but the advice here equally applies to other large shopping events.

What will Black Friday look like for me?

There are four main aspects to preparing for Black Friday:

- Designing the value offering for affiliates to promote
- Taking advantage of inbound opportunities
- Soliciting coverage for specific promotions
- Encouraging discovery of your products and offers

You have to show commitment

Large publishers receive many requests for coverage around key sale events, and they have high expectations for how they will perform. To pique their interest, you must provide a proposition that matches their goals and demonstrates you are just as serious about results.

Top tip

Create a permanent 'Black Friday Deals' page on your website. This can serve as a useful hub and landing page for customers and affiliates to find your best deals. Over time, it may also rank in the search engines, generating organic traffic and sales *without* having to pay affiliates.

Tenancies and paid placements

Demand outstrips supply around Black Friday, so the best coverage will likely have an additional fee.

As with any tenancy, you must weigh the pros and cons carefully. It's not possible for this book to tell you whether a particular tenancy is a great idea for your product or brand. However, there is one question that should be your guiding light: would the offer be a success without the tenancy?

The most important element of a Black Friday promotion is the strength and attractiveness of the offer. Tenancy coverage should amplify and elevate a deal - if you rely on the tenancy to define whether it was a success or a failure, it may not be the right time to invest.

What if I don't want to offer a Black Friday discount?

You don't have to participate in Black Friday if it doesn't help you meet your goals. However, it is a big part of the marketing calendar, so it is in your interest to try.

Customers are attracted to Black Friday because they feel they get extraordinary value for money during this period. This is usually achieved with a discount, but there are alternatives:

- A free or bundled product
- Loyalty points
- Extended support
- A discount on complementary accessories or products

The most important thing is to maximise the *perceived value*. Consumers and affiliates participate in Black Friday because they are looking for that 'what a bargain' moment.

Do good marketers really prepare six months early?

It is often said that good marketers prepare for Black Friday in May, Christmas in July, *etc.* Is that true? Are some advertisers and affiliates so organised that they know what they will be doing six months in advance?

It is safer to say you should *start* preparing well in advance, but preparation never really ends - advertisers and affiliates keep negotiating and booking activity until the last minute.

Many industries don't know what their prices and offers will be until very close to the event, so affiliates have to accommodate that. While they appreciate advance preparation, other factors affect their decision-making, like brand recognition and deal strength.

It certainly is not true that the best opportunities automatically go to the first people to ask. If that were the case, every marketer would simply book the next five years in advance.

You should start planning as soon as you are able, but don't feel bad if you don't have everything complete with three months to go.

Successful events tend to get longer

As an event becomes more influential, you can expect it to last longer than originally intended.

Black Friday and Cyber Monday were originally separate events before merging into Cyber Week. It's now not unusual to see Black Friday promotions extended to Christmas and beyond.

Other shopping events

There are far too many sales and events to list them all, so we'll concentrate on the larger ones for which affiliates usually offer exposure packages.

Boxing Day

December 26th

Boxing Day traditionally signals the start of the January sales. It is not as big as Black Friday, but it is still a significant shopping day, especially in the UK.

January sales

December 26th - January 31st

The traditional high street January sales made the transition to e-commerce very quickly.

Prime day

Mid-July

Prime Day is Amazon's largest shopping event. The exact date varies, but it is usually in July. While the official event is limited to the Amazon platform, other retailers often get in on the action with their own Prime Day discounts.

Back to School

September 1st

As the name suggests, this is the period in which students and their parents prepare for the approaching school year. Back to School week is often reinforced by heavy TV advertising for relevant brands, increasing consumer awareness and search traffic.

Singles' Day

November 11th

Singles' Day originated in China as an 'anti-Valentine's Day' and happens on 11th November because 11/11 represents four individuals standing together. It is huge in the Asian market, rivalling Black Friday, but we can expect it to spread across the globe, as Black Friday did.

Black Friday

First Friday after Thanksgiving - late November

Black Friday is the Friday after US Thanksgiving. Traditionally America's busiest shopping day, it is the largest online shopping event of the year.

Cyber Monday

Late November/early December

Cyber Monday started as an online alternative to the retail-focused Black Friday, but the two have now merged into a single period of sales and discounts. Black Friday/Cyber Monday spans four days, but it is common for retailers to offer discounts for a week or longer.

Panic Saturday/Super Saturday

Last Saturday before Christmas

This is the day when most single men start their Christmas shopping! Affiliates don't tend to offer coverage just for this day, but it is worth thinking about as the Christmas sale period draws to a close.

Offers and messaging based around gift wrapping and guaranteed delivery are particularly effective.

11.7 Newsletters

Email is the default way to communicate with your affiliates, and you can send an email to all your affiliates at any time from within your affiliate network.

Goals for this section
This section aims to equip you with good habits that ensure your routine affiliate communications and newsletters are fit for purpose.

What is an affiliate newsletter for?

A newsletter is your chance to inform affiliates about everything that may affect or enhance their promotional efforts. As an affiliate newsletter is sent to all of your enrolled affiliates, one email can have a big impact.

Newsletters can have several simultaneous goals:

- To achieve a specific outcome, such as highlighting current deals or offers
- To encourage all active, engaged publishers to keep up the good work
- To prompt inactive or lapsed affiliates to become active

New responsibility
Communicate regularly with your affiliates, providing information and resources they value in an easy-to-digest format.

How often should I email publishers?

Newsletter frequency depends on the availability of new, engaging topics. You should communicate with your affiliates as often as you have something worthwhile to communicate.

Build your own distribution list

Large affiliates often have several users with access to the same account. Email communications are typically sent to the 'main account contact', who may not be the correct recipient for regular promotional emails.

One way to get more control is to build your own distribution list, which will give you confidence that alerts and updates will reach the right person. A separate contact list also means you can treat your favourite or most valuable affiliates differently when you need to.

Affiliates usually respond positively when you ask, 'I keep a list of valued affiliates so I can contact them more easily - shall I add you?'

Don't forget important details

The most requested information is the expected end or expiry date of a promotion. This simple piece of information helps publishers understand the scope of the opportunity and whether it is compatible with their coverage.

Email communications should always answer the following questions:

- When does a promotion start and end?
- Is the product in the product feed?
- If you are advertising a sale or promotion, can the affiliate earn the normal commission rate?

You may not always be able to nail this information down, but affiliates will appreciate it if you at least try. You can always extend or amend the details when they are available.

Top Tip

Try to use accurate and descriptive subject lines - there is nothing worse than searching through 80 emails called 'newsletter' to find a specific piece of information.

Include the network, merchant ID and affiliate ID

Affiliates may work with dozens or even hundreds of merchants via several different affiliate accounts. It is up to you to make sure you can be identified to help the affiliate act on your communication straight away without having to work out who has contacted them.

You should always include:

- The network name (Webgains, Tradedoubler, Awin, etc.)
- Full merchant name
- Merchant ID
- Affiliate ID

Here is an email introduction that includes all the key pieces of information:

> 'Dear affiliate. I am contacting you about your affiliate activity on the QuikConnect 2000 partner program on Tradedoubler (Merchant ID 545), using the Affiliate Account ID 54636.'

If you regularly abbreviate your business name (for example, 'QuikConnect 2000' might become QC2000), an affiliate may not be able to find you using the network search function. Make sure you mention the full business name at least once and consider providing a hyperlink to your merchant profile so they don't have to search for you.

Pass on relevant bad news

You don't have to tell your affiliates every time something goes slightly wrong. It builds up negative sentiment, and you can be quite sure most affiliates won't return the favour.

However, if an outage affects the affiliates' ability to make money, you must inform them. This could be a good use for your tailored email list, which is a direct line to your most engaged, sale active affiliates.

11.8 Affiliate management agencies

Once you have launched your program, you will certainly be approached by several affiliate management agencies offering their services. Is it worth considering?

What are my options?

1. Manage the program yourself
2. Enlist an account manager at your affiliate network
3. Employ an external agency or affiliate management specialist

Pros and cons

✓ Relationships

Smaller programs often struggle to recruit the most influential partners. An agency with a long-standing relationship with larger publishers can help open those doors immediately.

✓ Insights

Agencies work on multiple campaigns in lots of different markets, putting them in an ideal position to identify trends and developments in the industry.

✓ Fresh eyes

A new set of eyes might bring different views and ways of thinking that could help develop your online marketing strategy.

✗ Costs

Most self-managed programs operate with a standard fee structure and a 30% override. As we discussed in the override and costs chapter, the final cost after VAT could be 56% higher than the commission you pay to affiliates. Can you afford to increase those costs further?

✓ Technology

Good agencies have a formidable understanding of attribution, tracking and the systems that support the affiliate marketing industry.

✗ Resources

Agencies are most effective when you can equip them with a budget to drive growth, which may not be possible at the self-managed stage.

If you are not able to take advantage of tenancies or paid media placements, then it may be too soon to recruit an agency.

✓ Experience

Agencies don't do anything you can't do yourself, but they might do it more quickly, more efficiently or in a different way.

✗ ROI

What you have to pay your agency for its services requires a certain level of sales and revenue to be worthwhile.

✓ Credibility

If your agency has a good reputation, it makes it easier for your program to be taken seriously.

Top Tip

It is very likely that you will be contacted by several affiliate management agencies when you first launch your affiliate program.

Think about how they found and contacted you – did they reach out with a well considered and researched proposition, or do they just send the same generic message to every new affiliate program that launches?

How big does my program need to be?

There is no definable point at which you should appoint an agency, and different agencies cater for different sized businesses.

As a rule of thumb, if the amount of revenue you would need to generate to justify the relationship is more than 30% of your current online sales, then you may not be ready to appoint an agency.

Summary

A dedicated agency is most suited for your affiliate program's **second stage** of growth.

When you shed the self-managed label and enter into a different contractual agreement with your network, you should be able to dedicate extra resources to fuel growth.

Watch this space

Self-managed programs are still a relatively new phenomenon, but they have already introduced thousands of new advertisers to the affiliate industry. Sooner or later, agencies will create offerings for this rich vein of potential clients, so keep an eye out for new, cost-effective ways to appoint and work with agencies.

11.9 Affiliate fraud

Affiliate marketing represents an opportunity for anyone to earn large amounts of money online. It is not surprising that it attracts the attention of people who are prepared to ignore the rules.

Goals for this section
This section will equip you to identify and investigate the types of affiliate fraud most likely to affect your self-managed program.

Affiliate fraud is as varied as the industry itself. This section will concentrate on the types of fraud that are most likely to affect self-managed affiliate programs rewarding affiliates on a CPS basis.

Cookie stuffing

Affiliate marketing relies on a range of tracking technologies collectively known as cookies. **Cookie stuffing** involves generating large amounts of cookies without the user's knowledge.

Cookie stuffing can be implemented using several different technologies of varying sophistication levels. Some methods can be identified by examining the source code of a web page, while others are essentially invisible.

Look out for

- High click volumes from seemingly poor-quality websites

Cookie replacement

Browser extensions, toolbars or malware can overwrite other publishers' cookies, directing commission from the correct affiliate to another, less deserving account.

While malicious extensions and toolbars usually perform a useful function in attracting users, their ultimate goal is to hijack the browsing experience to earn affiliate income and ad revenue. Some extensions replace affiliate links with their own, while others replace display and banner ads.

Look out for

- Very short lapse times between the
- Complaints from other affiliates
- Incomplete referrer information to indicate where a click or sale came from

Direct injection

Affiliate tracking is, by necessity, an open platform, which makes it easy for unscrupulous publishers to manipulate. Legitimate affiliate commissions are generated when the tracking script sends a signal to inform the affiliate network that a sale has occurred. Fraudsters can duplicate the tracking signal to register false commissions.

Look out for

- Orders that are reported in your affiliate network but can't be located in your e-commerce platform
- Incomplete referrer information to indicate where a click or sale came from

Human fraud

A lot of affiliate fraud is automated, but affiliate links can also be used by individuals or groups of people to generate commissions. This is often harder to spot because humans can easily circumvent fraud prevention measures.

Some common applications include:

- Completing orders using stolen identity and payment information
- Using affiliate links to monetise illegal telesales activity

Look out for

- A very high conversion rate - for example, one click, one sale
- An increase in complaints from customers
- Multiple sales from the same IP address
- Customers who say they ordered over the phone when you don't accept phone orders
- A high percentage of sales where the order is immediately cancelled or returned

Be alert, but don't panic unduly

We are addressing fraud through affiliate accounts because it pays to be thorough and well prepared, but fraud is not a widespread problem at this stage. Most self-managed programs are unlikely to be considered premium targets for fraudsters.

11.10 Don't forget

An affiliate program is a constantly evolving partnership. You will make a few mistakes along the way, and that is perfectly fine. To start you on your journey, here are a few things to remember and a few things to avoid.

Things to remember

You have a responsibility towards your affiliates

Your relationship with most publishers is a very casual contract. It is easy for a publisher to join your program and equally easy for them to leave. If you don't take your responsibilities to treat and reward publishers seriously, you will struggle to build meaningful relationships with them.

Pay on time

It is very important that affiliates receive commissions on a regular basis.

Self-managed programs have an advantage here - most affiliate networks insist on direct debit payments and auto-validation periods, which combine to ensure timely payments to affiliates.

Validate regularly

Most self-managed programs feature auto-validation, so you may be charged for invalid sales if you don't regularly check your orders.

Your PPC policy is important

PPC and affiliate marketing go hand in hand, and there are lots of PPC advertisers looking for new brands and products to promote. It is OK if you don't want to engage with PPC affiliates. However, this should be clearly explained in your program policies.

Affiliates assume the answer is yes until you tell them otherwise

Affiliates generally adopt the principle that it is better to ask forgiveness than to ask permission.

If you don't want affiliates to promote or represent you in certain ways, you *need to* communicate that. If your terms and conditions don't mention or forbid a specific type of activity, most publishers will assume it is permitted until they are told otherwise.

It is OK to pivot

As your business and affiliate program develops, you may notice it takes you in directions that you didn't expect. Sometimes these new developments may not be compatible with how you initially designed and configured your affiliate program.

While it isn't a decision that should be taken lightly, it is perfectly acceptable to change your program's fundamental proposition to meet these new demands.

That could involve changing commission rates or re-assessing the type of affiliates you work with. Any significant changes need to be managed carefully to maintain good relations with your publishers.

You should also liaise with your network to check your new proposition still fits your commercial agreement with them.

Affiliates may understand some terms differently

Depending on their experience, different affiliate professionals may interpret common terms in different ways. For example, if you approach an affiliate to say, 'would you be interested in rev-share?', they may not understand the term the same way you do. Don't rely on buzzwords - include a brief summary or example to make sure you are both on the same page.

Link discovery

You may send your best offers to your publishers or make them all available in your product feed, but that isn't the only way affiliates find links to promote. Every network makes it easy for affiliates to create links to any product or page on your website, and good affiliates will actively look for new promotion opportunities.

If there is a product or category that you would rather affiliates don't promote, then *let them know* that in your merchant description. Don't just assume they won't find the products.

Speak to other advertisers

Affiliate marketing is a thriving industry, with advertisers of all shapes and sizes who face the same challenges that you are.

That can be a wealth of information and experience, so keep an eye out for any chance to network with other advertisers.

There is not a strong online community for advertisers to interact, so events for affiliate marketing and the digital marketing industry are a good option, as are networking tools like Linkedin.

Regularly check your tech

Plug-ins and modern eCommerce platforms are more reliable than ever, but even then, tracking tags, product feeds, and reporting are rarely 'set and forget'.

The rest of the business and other external factors will conspire to break things, so check regularly

When a new development or change is introduced, ask yourself if it will affect your ability to track sales from affiliates and reward them for it

Long periods of downtime may irreparably sour the relationship (particularly with partners who use arbitrage, such as display, PPC or CSS) so maintaining these core functions is essential for a successful partnership.

Things to avoid

Never say 'we have no budget'

While this may be true at the time, it only serves to discourage affiliates and may harm relations in the future. It is better to say, 'we can't pay tenancies right now'.

Don't abandon your online profile

A lot of merchants neglect their online profile after their program has launched. Check your profile regularly and update it based on feedback and experience.

Duplicate content

Some affiliates re-use content from your website or network profile on their websites. Google and other search engines reward unique content and may penalise sites publishing content that they have seen before. Wherever possible, make sure the resources you provide to affiliates are unique. If you can't do this - for example, in your product feed - consider providing a truncated version to limit the risk.

Don't terminate affiliates unilaterally

There are lots of reasons to remove an affiliate from your program, but it should always be a considered decision. Unless you need to drastically change the direction of your program, each affiliate should be retained or removed on their merits, not *en masse*.

Don't share affiliates' activity or performance

Affiliates are innately interested in how well other publishers are performing and how they achieve those results.

Remember that your affiliates are in competition with each other, and your relationship with each publisher is a private agreement. You should never tell a publisher how another publisher is doing, or what their promotional activity looks like.

12: Regulations and compliance

Consumers are protected by a range of regulations that protect their online data and ensure they can trust what they discover online.

Goals for this chapter

While it isn't possible to thoroughly describe all relevant regulations, which are complex, this chapter should equip you with an understanding of the key issues and provides resources for further reading.

This chapter will cover:

Assumptions

This chapter assumes that your e-commerce business already complies with the appropriate regulations for e-commerce and data protection. You just need to update your policies and terms and conditions to reflect your new affiliate program.

12.1 The EU Omnibus Directive

The Enforcement and Modernisation Directive 2019/2161, or Omnibus Directive, is EU consumer rights legislation that came into effect in January 2020. It applies to merchants that sell or distribute to the EU.

Why is it relevant to retailers and affiliates?

The Omnibus Directive covers four main areas:

- New statutory consumer rights
- A code of conduct for online reviews and rules around fake reviews
- A process for verifying consumer reviews
- Changes to how discounts and price reductions are communicated

The final point is relevant here because it affects the prices you *and* your affiliates publish. It was introduced to help consumers understand what a discount is really worth.

New responsibility
Communicate sales and promotions to affiliate partners in a format compliant with the EU Omnibus Directive.

I'm in the UK

Since the United Kingdom has exited the European Union a lot of EU regulations will not be implemented in UK legislation, including the Omnibus Directive.

However, if you sell or ship goods or services to EU you do need to comply or risk legal action in member states.

It is also likely that UK specific legislation will be introduced in the future with the same fundamental goals.

Highlighting discounts or price reductions

Retailers have to show the lowest base price from the last 30 days, even if it wasn't the most recent price.

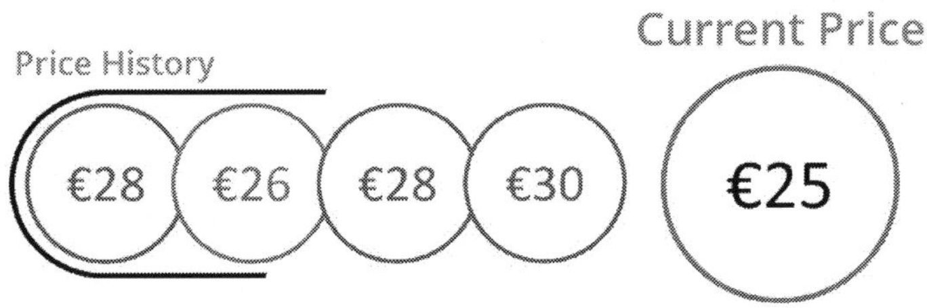

Outcome:
~~Was €26~~ **Now €25**

If a product was available for a lower price within the last 30 days, it cannot be presented as a discount.

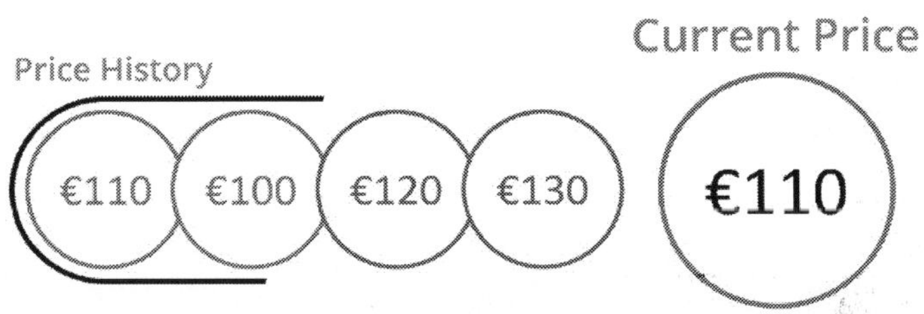

Outcome:
Should not be presented as a discount

These rules only apply to physical products, not digital services or content.

If you offer automated price changes for particular customers or groups

If your prices increase or decrease based on individual consumer data, such as their recent browsing history, purchasing history or age, this must be made clear to the consumer. Some technology enabler affiliates offer this feature, often called **dynamic pricing**.

I don't ship to the EU - can I follow the rules anyway?

There is nothing to stop anyone from following these rules if they feel it is in the interest of their customers.

You should check how any changes will affect how your deals are perceived if you work with price comparison partners or publishers who list discounts.

How do I implement this?

On-site

Most e-commerce platforms have been updated to comply with the Omnibus Directive. There is also a wide range of plug-ins available to help deal with these changes.

If a third party provides your product feeds for affiliates, PPC or CSS, you should speak to your technology provider to ensure you are within the regulations.

On your affiliates' sites

If your banners or creatives contain prices, make sure they are up to date and current.

If your product feed if contains 'sale' and 'previous' prices you should double-check that the logic of the Omnibus Directive is being applied

.

12.2 Disclosing affiliate links

Affiliates are rewarded for promoting and recommending your products, which means there could be conflicts of interest. Most online regulators have introduced rules about online endorsements to keep things fair.

Affiliates are responsible for disclosing their affiliate activity, but it is prudent to understand the rules and what they are for.

Where can I find the rules?

The UK and US publish comprehensive guidelines for online marketing, with specific examples for affiliate marketers. Guidance for some EU countries is less defined, but the International Chamber of Commerce (ICC), which is active in 43 territories, provides a good summary.

- UK: https://www.asa.org.uk/advice-online/affiliate-marketing.html
- US: https://www.ftc.gov/business-guidance/resources/ftcs-endorsement-guides-what-people-are-asking#affiliateornetwork
- Europe (ICC): https://iccwbo.org/publication/icc-advertising-and-marketing-communications-code/

Which rules should I follow?

Enforcement of the rules is based on the location of the audience, not the affiliate or merchant. If a UK-based affiliate is promoting to US-based consumers, then they should familiarise themselves with the US Federal Trade Commission (FTC) guidelines.

If your affiliates promote across Europe, the ICC guidelines are a good starting point. If your traffic comes from global partners, the US FTC regulations are the most stringent, so if an affiliate is FTC compliant, they *will likely* be compliant in other regions as well.

Who makes sure affiliates are compliant?

Affiliate networks seldom check publishers to make sure they have the appropriate disclosures - that is the affiliate's responsibility. The network terms and conditions usually stipulate that their affiliates are solely responsible for understanding and adhering to the regulations.

You should usually take the same approach, *except* when it could bring your brand into disrepute. If you are about to launch some significant coverage, there is no harm in asking the publisher to describe the steps they have taken to stay compliant.

Common sense summary

While you shouldn't have to monitor every partner for compliance, there are some basic guidelines you can pass on where appropriate.

Affiliates should:

- Clearly mark advertising activity as such
- Place a basic disclaimer on every page that features affiliate links
- Place the affiliate disclaimer in plain sight, not hidden out of the way
- Publish their full business name or trading name

If a publisher does these basic things, they are unlikely to bring unwelcome scrutiny to your affiliate program.

12.3 GDPR

The General Data Protection Regulation (GDPR) is a European privacy regulation that affects how websites collect, store and process information. It was announced in 2016, with full enforcement starting in May 2018.

If your website collects data about your visitors, you must make that clear to EU residents. It doesn't matter if your business or website is not located in the EU - if any of your visitors could be in the EU, you must be GDPR compliant.

In addition, GDPR specifies additional rights for visitors:

- Visitors must give consent for data collection
- They have the right to be forgotten
- They have the right to access their personal data
- Data must be stored in a secure environment
- Affected parties must be notified if there is a data breach

What is the risk?

Breaching the GDPR *could* lead to a fine of €20 million or up to 4% of your annual turnover.

The GDPR guidelines are open to interpretation, so the important thing is to do *something*. If you have made a reasonable effort to comply, you are unlikely to be penalised.

In practical terms, what do I have to do?

GDPR requires website owners to:

- Include a clear, GDPR-compliant cookie opt-in
- Display a concise, easy-to-understand privacy policy
- Describe the information that their website stores and collects
- Have a response plan in the event of a data breach

Most of the above requirements should already be in place to support your e-commerce activity. You just need to update a few pieces of information to cover your new affiliate program:

- Update your cookie opt-in to cover the third-party cookies created by your affiliate network
- Update your privacy policy
- Publish instructions on how visitors can delete local cookies or other tracking from their device under the right to be forgotten

Speak to your affiliate network - they should direct you to a GDPR resource with all the information you need.

New responsibility
Ensure that affiliate marketing is properly considered as part of your companies GDPR response.

13: In a nutshell

This book has covered building your proposition, technical integration, launching your program and managing your affiliates. That's quite a lot to take in, so here is a summary of all the key points, top tips and things to watch out for.

Congratulations, you are the proud owner of an affiliate program! Affiliate marketing is a great opportunity to reach new customers, and because it is **performance based**, you can try out new things without a large upfront investment.

You can set up a new program in a couple of hours, but the more time you spend considering the details, the better the results.

Your default proposition defines your first impression, so it should be easy to understand and make clear that working with you is an **opportunity to make money**.

It is usually very easy to add all the technical requirements to your website. Readily available plug-ins make it even easier for popular e-commerce platforms.

The more resources you provide, the more options you give your publishers. Some resources, like banners, are compulsory, while others, like product feeds, are optional. You should always make sure you can **properly support and maintain** anything you provide.

Self-managed programs are designed to be **accessible**, so advanced requirements, like multi-channel attribution, are not encouraged. For most advertisers and publishers, that is a good thing - it keeps things simple and reliable.

The **launch** is a key time for your program. Your online profile describes your program and explains why publishers should join. The more complete and enthusiastic you make your profile, the better.

New programs receive lots of applications from all over the industry. It is important to process these applications promptly - for the first few weeks of your program that means logging in every day.

It is completely up to you which applications you accept or reject. The two things to watch out for are **relevance** and **risk**.

You don't have to accept every application to your program, but affiliates can surprise you with their creativity and ingenuity. If in doubt, you can always **ask them** for more information.

As inbound applications slow down, it will be time to approach new partners to ask them to promote you. You can start this as soon as you feel ready.

Affiliates use all sorts of methods to promote advertisers. When this book describes sectors of the industry such as 'voucher codes' or 'cashback', it makes some sweeping generalisations. Specific affiliates may go against the grain or offer value that similar publishers don't.

If you **get the basics right,** you are setting up your affiliate program to succeed. That means you should:

- Approve affiliate applications promptly
- Validate sales consistently
- Communicate with your partners regularly

It is essential to reward affiliates fairly and consistently, which means paying affiliates as soon as possible.

Your validation process should be **safe and fair** for everyone concerned, including you. A commission is usually considered valid once payment has been taken, the order has been delivered, and the order can no longer be returned.

Top publishers may ask for tenancies or publish media packs listing coverage that they provide for an extra cost. Tenancies can be a shortcut to receiving extra coverage and can drive a lot of sales. Remember, though, that you are paying for coverage and traffic, not guaranteed results. **You are responsible** for making sure any exposure you secure converts into sales.

All networks provide tools for contacting your partners. You should use them regularly, but that doesn't stop you from building more direct relationships.

Every day in affiliate management is different, and as you experience the industry, you will meet publishers with ideas and opportunities that you never thought possible.

Through your new affiliate program you will meet publishers from a range of backgrounds and industries. Enjoy the interactions and take the opportunity to learn about their business and what they need to succeed.

More opportunities present themselves when your partners like and trust you.

14: What next?

Affiliate marketing is a great tool to reach new customers. All you need to do now is to work at it.

Go through the points in this book to make sure you have ticked off the big points and removed the biggest risks, then hit the emails, pick up the phone and speak to affiliates.

No program is perfect, so if there are some things in this book you can't address, don't worry. An actively managed program is better than one that is technically perfect and left to run itself. What matters is that you are thinking about your program, understanding how it works and keeping your eyes peeled for opportunities.

What if I outgrow my self-managed program?

With a lot of hard work and a little luck, your program may grow to a point where the commercial terms and 30% override no longer make sense.

Don't worry; that isn't a bad thing. Your network actively wants you to get to that point and will be more than happy to help you take the next step in the journey.

When you are ready, the network will discuss your options and help you transfer to a new arrangement. This will usually be a long-term contract with a fee structure that encourages more growth.

15: Acknowledgements

Producing this guide would not have been possible without the kind assistance of the following affiliate networks:

- Webgains
- Awin
- Tradedoubler

Many thanks to:

Steve Dean, Richard Dennys, Kevin Edwards, Niels de Groot, Ellen Kemp, Michelle O'Sullivan, Alona Malinovska, Seth Rubin and Corin Ward for your generous assistance.

Special thanks to the affiliate marketing community for their feedback and kind words:

Louis Sabet, Simon Mason, Rebecca Ellsmore, Anne Watson, Colin Carter, Brian Edwards, Boyce Marshall, Craig Mitchell, Tom Morgan and Matthew Rand.

Extra special thanks to David Paul Nixon for his sage editing advice.

This book was mainly written in Starbucks, Bracknell. Thank you to Naomi, Erin, Rob, Kaylie, Sophie and everyone else for the endless flow of delicious hazelnut lattes.

16: Appendices

16.1 External resources

A handy list of all the external resources referred to throughout this book.

Self-managed affiliate networks

Grow by Tradedoubler
https://grow.tradedoubler.com

Webgains Edge
https://www.webgains.com/public/en/webgains-edge-supports-smes-to-scale-up-with-affiliate-marketing

Awin Access
https://www.awin.com/gb/advertisers/awin-access

Influencer guidelines

UK: https://www.asa.org.uk/resource/influencers-guide.html

Global email regulations

https://en.wikipedia.org/wiki/Email_spam_legislation_by_country

Affiliate disclosure regulations

UK: https://www.asa.org.uk/advice-online/affiliate-marketing.html

US: https://www.ftc.gov/business-guidance/resources/ftcs-endorsement-guides-what-people-are-asking#affiliateornetwork

Europe (ICC): https://iccwbo.org/publication/icc-advertising-and-marketing-communications-code

GDPR

UK: https://ico.org.uk/for-organisations/guide-to-data-protection/guide-to-the-general-data-protection-regulation-gdpr

EU: https://ec.europa.eu/info/law/law-topic/data-protection_en, https://gdpr.eu

EU Omnibus Directive

EU: https://eur-lex.europa.eu/legal-content/EN/TXT/?uri=CELEX:32019L2161

Further reading

IAB Banner sizes:
https://www.iab.com/wp-content/uploads/2019/04/IABNewAdPortfolio_LW_FixedSizeSpec.pdf

E-A-T and YMYL SEO guidance:
https://www.searchenginejournal.com/on-page-seo/eat-ymyl

16.2 Summary of responsibilities

All of the responsibilities introduced throughout this book, collected together for easy reference.

Your Proposition

- Monitor the costs of your program to make sure you understand how much your affiliate sales cost your business.
- Regularly review your commission rates to ensure they are still fit for purpose, which is to reward partners fairly for driving new customers to your website.
- Communicate any changes to your proposition concisely and promptly to your affiliates.
- Keep your online profile up to date with the latest information about your proposition and the commission you pay.

Growing your program

- Review and process applications for your program regularly.
- Research and contact potential affiliates on a regular basis.
- Regularly review and contact inactive affiliates to persuade them to become active.

Resources you provide

- Make sure the image resources you provide are always up to date.
- Ensure that the affiliate tracking stays installed on your website and is not accidentally displaced or removed.
- Ensure that every product in your product feed is eligible for commission and that changes to stock or prices are promptly reflected in your feed.

Managing affiliates

- Make sure the affiliates that are enrolled to your program adhere to the rules and policies described in your online profile.
- Make sure affiliates are considered when you update or improve your website. Will the changes affect help or hinder their ability to earn commission?
- Research and understand the various options and support routes available for your self-managed program.

Processes

- Validate your sales regularly.
- Review and investigate TQs regularly.
- Make sure your processes and payment schedules enable customers to receive their cashback as quickly and smoothly as possible.
- When you do agree to pay tenancies, make sure they are paid promptly.
- Communicate regularly with your affiliates, providing information and resources they value in an easy-to-digest format.
- Find out which page(s) of your checkout cause a sale to track. It will be very useful in identifying and investigating possible tracking issues.

Regulations

- Communicate sales and promotions to affiliate partners in a format compliant with the EU Omnibus Directive.
- Ensure that affiliate marketing is properly considered as part of your companies GDPR response.

About the author

Steve Lownds has been an affiliate since 1997, and has been representing merchants since 2006. After leading flagship affiliate campaigns for leading global retailers, agencies and networks, he formed Multiplicit in 2020 to help advertisers of all sizes get the most out of affiliate marketing.

He has attended most affiliate events over the last 20 years, especially the ones with free sandwiches.

Printed in Great Britain
by Amazon

87234327R00165